What students are saying:

"Very happy with BeMo! They have done a great job preparing me for the MMI portion of residency interviews. They provide amazing constructive feedback that allows you to perform at your utmost potential. I would highly recommend this course to anyone that is looking for a way to perfect their interview skills. I worked with Karim and Helena, and they were both exceptional! They were very supportive and went out of their way to make sure I was scheduled for the time that worked best with my schedule. Overall, I felt that BeMo was engaged with my interview schedule and continuously focused on providing the best services possible. I wish the company a lot of success in the near future!" – Customer

"I am truly grateful to the staff and team at BeMo academic consulting IMG interview prep course for residency. Their commitment to my success was evident in the time and care they took in preparing me to showcase my best self for interviews. They helped provide me with the structure to answer questions to allow me to highlight examples of my experiences whilst also expressing my passion for the specialties I applied to. From MMI to standard panel, USA to Canada, BeMo was prepared." – Simi

"As an IMG, I matched to one of my top 5 residency choices, in internal medicine!! There is no doubt that BeMo was of great assistance throughout my application season, as I cultivated and developed my professional interview skills. All were consultants were wonderful, but three were most

notable in my journey, namely (1) Peter, (2) Matthew, and (3) Samuel. I highly recommend their service." – Keir

"My experience with BeMo was nothing short of remarkable. I subscribed to their platinum program to help me prepare for residency interviews in CaRMS. Although expensive, the platinum program was extremely helpful because I was able to practice as much as needed for my interviews. The consultants were excellent and knew exactly how to help you prepare for the interviews. I used their feedback religiously and my interview performance improved in a very short time. It was all worth it because I matched to Oncology in Queen's! I would strongly recommend that if you need help with interview preparation, look into BeMo!" – Customer

"My experience was the perfect amount of practice, feedback and positive encouragement needed for my last second interview as an Internal Medicine candidate. In the span of ~1.5 hours, we went through a thorough mock interview, reviewed my answers and he went above and beyond in answering some of my more candid questions towards his thoughts/opinions. Before I signed up at BeMo Academic Consulting, I fully admit of balking due to the price but fully endorse the level of professionalism and honesty provided in helping me polish my interviewing capabilities." – Roland

"Brad was extremely helpful! He was professional, honest, eloquent and provided me with very useful feedback and tips! This practice interview has given me confidence for my upcoming interview, and now I know what areas need improvement, and he definitely helped me polishing my answers! Thank you so much!" – Customer

"Being a foreign graduate, I was struggling to prepare great responses to interview questions. More importantly, didn't have much idea how I am performing. Then I found BeMo, it has been tremendously helpful so far. The mock interview sessions and the feedback I have received from the consultants have been awesome! Now I have a much clearer concept of what to expect during the interview and how to appropriately respond. I hope with more sessions and practice I will have the confidence to do well and get a residency position!" – Customer

"I used BeMo's gold program for residency interview prep, as well as their MMI resources in my journey to getting back to Canada as a CSA who studied in Hungary. I found the MMI resources very useful for organizing my thoughts in a coherent manner, and a lot of the skills I developed from there translated to improved interview skills. I had a subscription for the MMI *simulator as well, but I found this resource underwhelming because it was difficult for me to stay engaged with the large gaps in between stations. For the gold package I worked with Adam for one session for MMI prep, and Allen for two one on one prep sessions. I felt that these definitely helped fine tune my responses and make them more cohesive, particularly the one on one preparation sessions as they were tailored to the school I was applying to. I'm very happy to say that I matched into my first choice of Internal Medicine at Western University. Thanks for your help in my journey back home Adam and Allen, and the team at BeMo." –* Gurjot

"Excellent experience with BeMO for residency interview prep. Sessions are very helpful, personalized and provide great feedback for improvement. Would recommend!" – Customer

"Great first session for residency practice interviews. There were a number of small details that were sabotaging my ability to come across competently. I had a particular issue that I've had to address in my interviews so far and got great feedback as to how to frame it in way that people would feel satisfied with the progress I've made." – Customer

"I completed my interview course and my real interview. The interview course is extremely helpful. The feedback I got from each session helped me prepare each time. Thank you BeMo!" – Unnati

"I have used BeMo academic consulting while I was preparing for medical residency interviews in Ontario. Their service was very satisfying, punctual and helpful. I recommend it for IMGs who have no idea where to start from." – Hisham

"An excellent simulation of real residency interview. Structured questionnaire with thorough point to point clear and personalized feedback. Highly recommended before any interview." – H.B.

"I used two mock interview sessions and they were very helpful. Both tutors were on time, polite, concerned, and gave me detailed feedback on my positives and on my areas of growth opportunity. It made a difference on my residency interviews and I definitely recommend them!" – Monica

BeMo's Ultimate Guide to Residency Interview

How to Ace Your Residency Interview without Memorizing Any Sample Questions

BeMo® Academic Consulting Inc.

Important Notice. Please read carefully. By using this book, you acknowledge that you have read, understood, and agreed with our terms and conditions below.

Disclaimer: Please note that certain parts of this book are similar or identical to the content presented in BeMo's interview video training course and BeMo's Ultimate Guide to Multiple Mini Interview (MMI). Although certain parts of this book are completely new material, you will have access to most of the content presented if you have purchased any of the programs or books above. Furthermore, if you have purchased any of our CASPer prep video training, programs, or book, you will also notice some similarities. This is because CASPer and the MMI were created by the same university and are thus very similar. Nevertheless, there are many differences which we have highlighted in this book. Moreover, doing well on CASPer does not necessarily translate to doing well on MMI and vice versa. You may choose to use this book as a starting point in your preparation or as a complement to our MMI programs at your discretion.

We have conducted thorough research to provide accurate information to help you prepare for and ace your residency interview. However, readers are responsible for their own results and must always adhere to official interview instructions.

BeMo is not affiliated with, nor does it endorse, any of the organizations mentioned, including, but not limited to universities, colleges, official test administrators, or any external websites, unless explicitly indicated otherwise.

Score increase claims refer to score increases observed in practice simulations.

Copyright: The content of this book is the copyright of BeMo Academic Consulting Inc. All rights reserved. Any use, reproduction, in part or in entirety, without the written consent of BeMo Academic Consulting Inc. is strictly prohibited.

Trademarks: BeMo is the legal owner of various trademarks, tradenames, logos, and phrases. These include the tradename "BeMo®", trademarks "CASPer SIM™", "MMI SIM™", "Get In Or Your Money Back®", "BeMo 100% Satisfaction Guarantee™" and

CONTRIBUTING AUTHORS

Dr. Behrouz Moemeni, Ph.D., founder & CEO of BeMo

Ms. Ronza Nissan, M.A., admissions expert & lead trainer

Dr. Meng Yang, Ph.D., admissions expert & associate lead trainer

EDITORS

Dr. Diana Fernandez, Ph.D., admissions expert

Want a FREE sample
residency simulated mock
interview?

Go to
SampleResidencyInterview.com

Would you like us to help
you ace the residency interview?

Go to
BeMoResidencyInterview.com

Contents

Acknowledgments

We would like to thank our students and their parents for putting their trust in us and giving us the privilege of being a part of their journey. You have inspired us and taught us lessons we would not have learned on our own. Thank you for your continued support and for investing in our mission. You are the reason we get up in the morning.

We would like to thank the countless number of admissions deans, directors, officers, pre-health advisors and school counselors who have 'unofficially' supported our mission. Thank you for encouraging us and, most importantly, thank you for making us think critically. We appreciate what you do, and we understand the impossible task you face each and every single day.

A huge thanks to our team members, both past and present. BeMo wouldn't be what it is today without you.

And, of course, a huge thanks to our family and friends who have been unconditionally supportive, even when we couldn't spend as much time with them because of our obsession with our mission here at BeMo.

Foreword

First, CONGRATULATIONS for making the commitment to educate yourself to become a competitive applicant, a better person, and a better future professional. The fact that you have purchased this book tells us that you understand the value of continuous learning and self-improvement. The world rewards individuals who continuously seek to educate themselves because *knowledge is power*. Before we dive in, let's get on the same page about the purpose of this book, who this book is for, who it is NOT for, and why you should listen to us. But first, a few words from our founder and CEO, Behrouz Moemeni.

Why I Founded BeMo®: Message from BeMo's Founder and CEO, Dr. Behrouz Moemeni

Sometimes you must do what's necessary, even if the chances of success are slim to none. Students often ask me what gets me up in the morning and what motivated me to found BeMo. The answer for me is rather simple and has remained the same since day one.

I started BeMo with my cofounder, Dr. Mo Bayegan, in 2013 – see why it's called "BeMo" now? Our partnership began when we first met back in high school in 1996, and then later solidified during our undergraduate and graduate years.

We both felt every student deserves access to higher education, whatever his or her social status or cultural background, because education is the best way to introduce positive change in our world.

Sadly, I believe most of the current admissions practices, tools and procedures are biased, out-dated, and more importantly, scientifically unproven. Therefore, in 2013, as Mo and I were finishing our graduate studies, we decided to create BeMo to make sure no one is treated unfairly due to flawed admissions practices.

At the time, I was finishing my Ph.D. studies in Immunology at the University of Toronto, which was a transformational educational experience. I had the privilege of working with one of the sharpest minds in the field, Dr. Michael Julius. He taught me many things over the years, but two lessons stayed with me: 1) There is tremendous value in having curiosity about scientific or technological innovations to seek the truth rather than confirm one's own opinions, and 2) what you do has to be the reason that gets you up in the morning. Though I wasn't his best student, I was still relatively successful. I won 19 awards, I was invited to 7 international conferences, and I even had an unsolicited job offer before I had defended my thesis. The job would give me a secure source of income and I would have been able to start paying my mounting student debt, but I ultimately decided to abandon a career in academia. Instead, I chose to start BeMo. Despite having many well-established competitors and an overall slim chance of success, I felt – and I still do to this day – that the mission was well worth the risk. I truly believe what we do here at BeMo adds more value to each of our students' lives than anything else I could have done in academia, and I would not trade it for the world.

Over the years, our amazing and steadily growing team has helped many students navigate the admissions process. We really couldn't have done it without them, and it's been a privilege to teach with them and learn from them over the years. (Thanks for sticking with us!)

We are aware that our methods are controversial in some circles; innovative ideas often are. However, we are confident in our belief – and the scientific literature supports this – that current admissions practices are rife with bias and must be improved.

This is why, in 2017, I founded another independent company called SortSmart®, which has created what I consider to be the fairest, most scientifically sound, and cost-effective admissions screening tool out there. I invite you to visit SortSmart.com to learn more and tell your university admissions office to bring SortSmart to your school.

In the meantime, while SortSmart is gathering momentum, we, at BeMo, will continue to support students just like you to make sure no group of students is treated unfairly. You can rest assured that we will not stop until our goals have been achieved.

To your success,

Behrouz Moemeni, Ph.D.

CEO @ BeMo

A bit about us: BeMo Academic Consulting (BeMo)

We are an energetic academic consulting firm, comprised of a team of researchers and professionals who use a proven, evidence-based, and scientific approach to help prospective students with career path development and admissions to undergraduate, graduate, and professional programs such as medicine, law, dentistry, and pharmacy.

We believe your education is one of your most valuable assets and learning how to become a great future professional or scholar doesn't need to be complicated. We also believe that each student deserves access to higher education, regardless of his or her social status or cultural background. However, most of the current admissions practices, tools, and procedures are biased, outdated, and more importantly, scientifically unproven.

Our goal is to create truly useful (and scientifically sound) programs and tools that work and provide more than just some trivial information like the other admissions consulting companies out there. We want to make sure everyone has a fair chance of admission to highly competitive professional programs despite current biases in admissions practices.

We do whatever it takes to come up with creative solutions and then test them like mad scientists. We are passionate about mentoring our students, we're obsessed with delivering useful educational programs, and we go where others dare not to explore.

Why should you listen to us?

We are the leaders in admission preparation for extremely competitive professional schools. Each year, we help thousands of students gain admission to top schools around the world by assisting them with their application documents and preparing them for CASPer and interviews of all styles, including Multiple Mini Interviews (MMIs), traditional interviews, and video interviews. We have an exceptional team of practicing professionals, medical doctors, scholars, and scientists who have served as former interview evaluators and admissions committee members. Learn more about our experts at BeMoAcademicConsulting.com.

What we are about to share with you in this book is based on what we learned in our sought-after paid training programs. What we offer works and it works consistently. In fact, research has shown that our programs can increase applicants' application scores by up to 27% in simulated interviews. Our programs are in high demand and we are certain they will also work for you.

Why did we write this book?

There is so much misinformation surrounding the admissions process, from online forums to university clubs, and even some university guidance counselors and official test administrators. While some of this information is well-intended, the level of inaccuracy is astounding. In particular, the credibility of online forums can be called into question because it is not clear who the authors are or what motivations they have. These forums are frequently filled with fake profiles, some of them official university administrators and test administrators trying to control the flow of information so only their version of 'facts' is distributed. To make matters worse, some of these forums offer sponsorship opportunities to companies, which puts them in a financial conflict of interest. Also be wary of information from most student clubs because, again, these organizations frequently form financial relationships with companies to garner support for their operations and, as a result, receive and distribute one-sided information. Additionally, most books available are incomplete and tend to have a narrow focus on teaching you interview 'tricks', without offering any meaningful strategy on how to ace any possible *type* of interview question. They do not focus on the big picture that is essential to your success, both as an applicant and as a future practicing professional.

What is this book about?

This book is about helping you develop the fundamental tools so you can become a mature, ethical, and knowledgeable individual, which is essential to your future profession. While we spend a considerable amount of time walking you through how to prepare for your residency interview, it is important to always remain focused on the big picture.

Who is this book for and who is it NOT for?

If the residency program you are applying to requires you to participate in an interview, then this book is perfect for you. Regardless of where you are in your preparatory process, this book has something for you, provided that you are willing to put in the hard work and invest in yourself. Getting into a competitive residency program is challenging, as is becoming a practicing professional. The journey is also very consuming of your time, money, and energy.

We do *not* share any quick 'tricks', 'shortcuts', or 'insider scoops' like some of the other books you may find because:

a) You cannot trick your way to becoming a mature, ethical professional. Rather, you must put in long hours of self-training. If a professional athlete must train for years – on average ten years, hence the 'ten-year rule' – to get to that level of proficiency, wouldn't it make sense that our future doctors, lawyers, dentists, and pharmacists, who deal with people's lives, would need to put in the effort to learn the necessary skills?

b) Sharing 'tricks' or 'insider scoops' would be highly unethical. You should be immediately alarmed if a book or admissions company claims to be sharing 'insider' information.

c) We have a strict policy at BeMo to only help students who are genuinely interested in becoming caring professionals who want to serve their communities, not those who may be primarily motivated by financial security, status, or social pressure from their parents and peers, and certainly not those who are looking for an easy, cheap shortcut to get in.

How should you read this book?

We recommend that you first read the book cover to cover and then come back to specific chapters for a detailed read. The more you read the book, the more you will internalize the essential strategies. It is important to note that there is a lot of information in this book, and if you try to do everything at once, it may be overwhelming and lead to discouragement. Therefore, it is best that you first read this book for pleasure from cover to cover, then gradually start to implement our recommendations.

To your success,
Your friends at BeMo

CHAPTER I

What is a Residency Interview?

The residency interview is often the last and most dreaded step prior to the anticipated day you are matched with a program. You are invested in your residency application journey and have worked hard to get to this stage. You have sacrificed time spent with family and friends and your weekends to work on core clerkship rotations and ace your board exams. You have probably spent hundreds of collective hours shadowing physicians, arranging electives, and getting reference letters. So, isn't all that enough? Unfortunately, the answer is no. You know very well that residency programs receive enormous numbers of applications each year, and with such limited seats in their specialty training programs, you need to perform at your best to clear this last hurdle.

This is where we come in to help. Whether you are still finalizing your residency applications and planning in advance, waiting for interview invitations, or have confirmed your interview dates, we are here to walk you through the interview preparation. We will break down practice strategies, both general and specific, and go through the interview types residency programs use. However, before we do that, we need to first understand the history of interviews in the selection of candidates for professional programs.

History and Rationale Behind the Use of Residency Interviews

Where exactly did the practice of interviewing applicants for residency positions come from? Up until the late 1970s, all residency programs worked in the same way: a student would graduate from medical school and complete a rotating intern year at a hospital where they cycled through every specialty. At the end of that year, they would either become a general practitioner or enter a residency program to become a specialist. Since the 1980s, however, specialties, including family medicine (which used to be called general practice), have formalized their application systems. Today, students generally apply through a centralized system, such as the Electronic Residency Application Service (ERAS) in the U.S. or the Canadian Resident Matching Service (CaRMS) in Canada, to various specialty programs in their last year of medical school. Upon completion of the program, which could last 2 to 5 years (sometimes more!), residents become board-certified in a specialty like family medicine, internal medicine, psychiatry, general surgery, and so forth.

Since the number of medical students has increased, so too has the number of applicants to residency positions. Residency programs have become more competitive, and the interview has become increasingly common over time to the point that they are now an integral part of the selection process no matter which program or specialty you apply to. Since these interviews tend to be modeled after medical school interviews, let's take a closer look at the history of medical school interviews. Although interviews are adapted to fit the needs of each program, they all share the same history and rationale.

The first medical school, Schola Medica Salernitana, was founded in the 9th century in southern Italy. Their admissions criteria were based entirely on the financial status of the applicants – those who could afford eight years of medical training – rather than previous academic success, critical reasoning, or interpersonal skills. Although finances determined admissions, Schola Medica Salernitana published several guides on how to treat patients respectfully – including guides for patient care and bedside manner. This indicates that, since the inception of medical training, the healthcare profession has always valued patient care, regardless of admissions criteria.

Hundreds of years later, in 1765, the University of Pennsylvania established the Perelman School of Medicine, the first medical school in North America. The Perelman School of Medicine, and other institutions that opened around that time, maintained the basic principles established by Schola Medica Salernitana – the importance of serving others and equal emphasis on both technical and interpersonal skills. However, wanting to train students who already had the foundations necessary the complete their studies, early North American medical schools based their admission criteria on previous academic success, leaving students' interpersonal skills to be developed during medical school training.

In the 1920s, standardized testing was first included in the admissions process. The original test, created by F.A. Moss and colleagues, was initially called the "Moss Test" and thought to be a measure of readiness for medical school. It was later revamped and renamed as the Medical College Admissions Test, commonly known as the MCAT. The rise in standardized testing led to the incorporation of board exams, such as the United States Medical Licensing Examination (USMLE) and the Medical Council of Canada Qualifying Examination (MCCQE), for selecting medical professionals. Scores from Parts 1 and 2 of the USMLE are now included in medical students' applications to residency programs in the U.S. In Canada, since board exams are not completed until after the candidate is matched, no part of the MCCQE is included in the application to Canadian residency programs.

Unfortunately, accepting students based on standardized testing and academic history resulted in attrition rates as high as 50% amongst medical students. As if to make matters worse, medical schools initially responded by increasing academic requirements. The focus on numeric performance in selecting medical professionals finally began to shift in the late 1990s and early 2000s when professional regulatory bodies of medicine began conducting studies to understand the major complaints the public had about their health care professionals. In a study published in the *New England Journal of Medicine*, it was revealed that the number one complaint most patients had about their physicians was not with regard to their clinical skills and competencies, but rather with the doctors' emotional intelligence and soft skills (N Engl J Med 2005; 353:2673-2682). Patients complained that their doctors were not compassionate or empathetic enough, or simply did not have good communications skills. Based on this evidence, professional faculties were tasked with devising admissions procedures that selected candidates who not only had a great academic record, but also possessed strong soft skills.

Thus, many professional faculties began utilizing various tools to find appropriate candidates who possess strong non-cognitive skills such as communication skills, teamwork, empathy, critical thinking, ethical decision-making, interpersonal skills, and professionalism. The evaluative tools that were initially introduced included the personal statement, autobiographical sketch, short essays, and the traditional interview. Though the traditional interview is still used by many institutions, other interview formats have evolved and become increasingly popular. The following is a list of the formats you may encounter at your residency interview:

- Traditional one-on-one interview
- Panel interview
- Multiple Mini Interview (MMI)
- Hybrid interview (a combination of Traditional and MMI)
- Virtual or video interview

We will take a close look at each of them in *Chapter V: Different Types of Residency Interviews*, noting how they are structured, who the evaluators are, and the rationale behind using them.

In summary, residency application processes have evolved over time to provide better insight into an applicant's academic and professional suitability. Interviews are now a key component of your application to your specialty and program of choice. In some ways, we haven't really come that far from the principles of Schola Medica Salernitana: Serve others with both technical proficiency and interpersonal skills. These principles have been followed since ancient times, predating the establishment of medical schools and institutions. Though you do not need to know the earliest details of the history of medicine, it is important to understand the founding principles that have always guided medical practice. While the science of medicine has transformed and will continue to evolve, the values that doctors must uphold have remained virtually unchanged.

What are admissions committees looking for?

As we discussed above, residency programs do not rely simply on your grades, board exam, or other test scores. They are looking for non-cognitive skills which are important for practicing physicians to have.

What types of skills are they looking for? We mentioned some of them above, but here they are again so you can review them at any time:

- Communication skills, both written and verbal
- Collaboration and teamwork
- Management abilities, including the management of others and the self (i.e., time and stress management)
- Leadership and decision-making while maintaining a collaborative atmosphere
- Advocacy skills, especially speaking up for vulnerable or underserved individuals and populations
- Empathy and compassion
- Altruism, the ability to put others' needs before your own
- Reliability, dedication, perseverance, and hard work
- Critical-thinking and problem-solving abilities

OK, that's a long list! The good thing is that you likely already have most of these abilities and qualities, as they are very similar to the ones that medical schools evaluated you on when you applied, and you probably continued to develop these during your medical education.

What is left to do is to effectively showcase them, just as you did on your medical school interview. Of course, the competition now consists of other medical students, so this final part just got harder!

At this stage, it is important to reflect on and consider which specialty and program you have applied to. Although all of the skills listed above are important for all the specialties, different specialties may value certain qualities over others. For example, psychiatrists highly value communication and empathy, as well as advocacy. Internal medicine, being a research-intensive field, may value critical thinking and problem-solving. Pediatrics surely emphasizes collaboration and empathy. Think carefully about the rotations you have done and the qualities shown by your preceptors and other health care professionals, and reflect on how they coincide with your own traits and skills.

How reliable are these interviews?

Now, you may be wondering how effectively these skills can be assessed using interviews. We will therefore take some time to explore the reliability and validity of this assessment tool. (Note that most research on this topic was conducted on medical school applicants given the comparatively larger subject pool. However, the results can be extrapolated to all professional interviews.)

There is some evidence that interview assessments are *reliable*. That is to say, results are somewhat consistent across multiple tests over time. For example, research by Dahlin and colleagues (2012) shows that candidates who are selected by both their interview and academic performances, rather than their academic qualifications alone, perform better on future clinical examinations like the objective structured clinical examination (OSCE).

However, the validity of interview assessments has been called into question. Unlike the evaluation of hard skills in standardized tests, the evaluation of soft skills is qualitative and subjective. Therefore, regardless of which interview format is used, there will always be a question of how accurately applicants are being assessed. Many factors can influence applicants' interview ratings. Obviously, one of these is the difference between the competency of applicants themselves, but differences between the interviewers can also contribute to the variation in scores. These differences include, but are not limited to, inconsistent interviewer training, distinct interviewer experiences or backgrounds, and their longstanding (subconscious) biases. In particular, these biases can lead evaluators to make quick decisions and to selectively search for evidence to support their judgment, rather than evaluating all information equally and rating interviewees objectively. Ideally, differences between the applicants should account for most of the variance in their interview outcomes, but in a study published in 1996, researchers Harasym and colleagues found that the variability between interviewers can account for up to 56% of the total variance in interview ratings! Therefore, even medical schools and residency programs should be careful about the conclusions they draw from interviews alone.

Furthermore, two independent SortSmart studies on medical school admissions in the U.S. and Canada showed that *all* interview types used as admissions screening tools are more likely to select applicants from higher-income families. The results from U.S. schools are given in Figure 1.

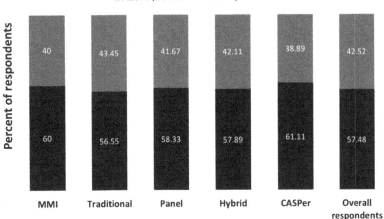

The Wealthy are Most Represented

Figure 1. Students from families with an annual income greater than $80,000 represent the majority of successful applicants across all interview types. Printed with permission from SortSmart Candidate Selection Inc.

Figure 1 shows that candidates from families with annual incomes of $80,000 or more make up the majority of successful candidates across all interview formats and the CASPer test. This income distribution is concerning because it is not representative of the overall pool of applicants, in which there is no significant difference between the number of students from families earning below $80,000 per year and those from families earning above that threshold. It is also not representative of the American population, for which the median household income is approximately $60,000 per year, according to the U.S. Census Bureau. Though the connection is not certain, the bias from interviews and CASPer may stem from their use of situational judgment tests (SJTs) which also present the same bias (see below).

Do Situational Judgment Tests *Really* Work?

Situational judgment tests (SJTs) place applicants in hypothetical scenarios and allow interviewers to evaluate their approaches and behaviors. The assumption is that this method reveals applicants' true motivations and behavioral tendencies in real life situations. It is a methodology that has existed for decades and is currently used not only in MMIs and CASPer tests (MMI's online sister), but also in traditional, panel, and hybrid interviews.

However, we have identified a number of problems with SJTs:

Problem #1

The use of hypothetical scenarios forces applicants to respond unnaturally to hypothetical situations. They know that their response should be one that is socially acceptable. Therefore, instead of reflecting on what they *really* would do, applicants tend to say what they think is the 'right' answer. This means these tests might not be able to detect the true personality of applicants; they merely detect how attuned applicants are to social norms.

Problem #2

SJTs are biased against certain populations. Reports indicate that SJT scores tend to be lower for applicants with lower socioeconomic status, male applicants, and those from underrepresented minorities. We direct you to the following links for two of these studies:

https://www.ncbi.nlm.nih.gov/pubmed/26017355

https://www.ncbi.nlm.nih.gov/pubmed/28557950

Applicants from higher socioeconomic backgrounds are better at formulating socially acceptable responses due to their upbringing and socialization. Judging the appropriateness of a response to a very delicate or stressful hypothetical scenario can vary across cultures. These tests are singularly guided by accepted western cultural norms. This can pose significant challenges to non-native applicants, new immigrants, or those who are immersed in another culture. The diverse makeup of the population in the U.S., the U.K., Australia, and Canada, for example, makes this a significant barrier for applicants.

Problem #3

SJTs are often said to be 'immune to test preparation', a claim we find difficult to accept. Personal and professional behaviors are learned, not inherited; a parent, teacher, or coach can absolutely teach these skills to an individual. In fact, in *Chapter III: Top 2 Myths about Residency Interview Preparation*, we discuss evidence showing that coaching can and does impact performance on these types of tests.

Problem #4

SJTs scores have not been shown to correlate with actual job behavior. The best correlation data to date is problematic in several ways: 1) It shows a correlation between test scores and future performance on medical licensing examinations, not job performance. 2) It is self-reported by the creators of the for-profit companies selling these products. 3) The correlation itself is weak, accounting for only about 16% of the variance in performance. Imagine going to a doctor who claimed to be able to make a correct diagnosis 16% of the time! Thus, we have no evidence showing that SJTs are a reliable way to evaluate which applicants will make great practicing professionals.

Problem #5

SJTs cannot measure each candidate's level of intrinsic motivation. Unlike test scores or grades, motivation directly impacts behavior. A motivated student is one who wants to improve themselves without outside direction or pressure and will work hard to become the best medical professional they can be. Furthermore, motivation is not correlated with gender, race, or socioeconomic status. Thus, it is a trait that should be evaluated, but isn't, and certainly not by SJTs.

We have now outlined the history and rationale behind the use of interviews for residency applicants, touched on the types of interviews you may encounter, and taken a closer look at how reliable and useful (or not!) these interviews really are. Despite the fact that interviews may not accurately identify the skills and qualities that make a great physician, they are (for now) widely used as a screening tool, so you must still be able to do well on yours to achieve admission to a residency program.

Moving forward, we will debunk myths and look at facts related to your interview performance, and take a closer look at both the types of interviews mentioned briefly in this chapter and the different question types you will likely encounter on interview day.

CHAPTER II

Admissions Statistics and Why You Must ACE Your Residency Interview

E ach school uses your interview score in the way they see fit when deciding the ranking of applicants. The best way to find out this information is to consult the official admissions website or to contact the admissions office. Regardless, your interview performance is likely going to be a significant factor, if not *the* determining factor of how well you rank compared to other applicants.

To give you a more concrete idea of how important the interview is in the residency application process, let's consider the results from the 2018 National Residency Matching Program's (NRMP) survey of program directors, which was intended to elucidate the factors these directors used to rank candidates before and after the interview.

(Note that while these results are from U.S. medical schools, the statistics should be fairly similar for Canadian programs.)

In this survey, 39 post-interview factors were ranked based on 1) the percentage of programs citing it as a factor they considered, and 2) the importance of the factor on a scale of 1 to 5. The following are the highest ranked factors:

a) Interactions with faculty during the interview and visit (cited by 96% of directors, rating = 4.8)

b) Interpersonal skills (cited by 95% of directors, rating = 4.9)

c) Interactions with house staff during the interview and visit (cited by 91% of directors, rating = 4.8)

d) Feedback from current residents (cited by 86% of directors, rating = 4.7)

Factors (a) and (c) are quite obviously interview-related. The scores you receive based on factors (b) and (c) can, of course, be informed by interactions you had with individuals outside of the interview or by other parts of your application. However, you can be fairly certain that current residents will be basing their feedback heavily on how they perceive you during your interview visit, and that your interpersonal skills will be the number one consideration. The remaining 35 factors (e.g., board exam scores, letters of recommendation, and so forth) are all cited by less than 80% of program directors and given importance scores of 4.1 or lower.

Overall, according to this survey, an average of 856 candidates submitted applications to the various residency programs. Out of these 856 candidates, an average of 119 candidates were invited to an interview. Out of these 119 interviewees, 77 were eventually ranked for the Match. Because of the incredibly limited availability of positions in each program, less than 1% of the candidates who originally applied to a specific residency program would have gained a position. Of course, these are average figures for all residency programs, but these numbers should give you an indication of how competitive this process can be. You must therefore *ace* your interview to have any chance at successfully matching with your desired program.

Now that we have established the importance of the interview in the application, we can begin to lay the foundations for good interview preparation practices. As a first step, the next chapter will reveal and disprove two common myths about the process to help you avoid unnecessary setbacks.

Are you ready?

CHAPTER III

Top 2 Myths about Residency Interview Preparation

The general conclusion you have probably come to by now is that the residency interview is not going to be so easy. While that is true, we are going to do everything we can in the next few chapters to equip you with the tools necessary to succeed.

One thing that makes this process exceedingly difficult to navigate is the plethora of misinformation about how to prepare, which can set you off-course from your intended goals, in this case, acing your interview. That is why we have dedicated this chapter to dispelling two common myths about the preparation process so that you can avoid these pitfalls.

Myth #1: "There are no right or wrong answers."

This is a statement about interviews you might hear that sometimes even appears on official program websites. While it may sound plausible given the open-endedness of many interview questions, it simply cannot be true. If it were true, everyone would get matched, regardless of their performance at their interview, which would make the entire exercise an extravagant waste of everyone's time. At best, this statement is dangerously misleading, causing many applicants to underprepare for and fail their interviews. In reality, although there are no *specific* right or wrong answers to the interview questions you will encounter, there are certainly appropriate and inappropriate answers. That is, there is a marked difference between a well-thought-out, mature, professional, and articulate response, and one that is immature, unprofessional, and disorganized. It is your job to put in the effort and time to learn how to do the former and avoid the latter. Otherwise, not matching to any program your interviewed for is as likely as the rising sun.

Myth #2: "You can't prepare in advance."

This is the most common and absurd myth about interviews, one that is, sadly, also promoted on some official program websites. This assessment tool has been claimed to test personal and professional characteristics such as empathy, communication, and ethics, all of which are *learned* behaviors. Nobody is *born* with any of these.

You and other students who are participating in our interview preparation programs likely do not need to be convinced of this. Clearly, you have picked up this book and/or signed up for our programs because you believe there is something tangible you can do to improve your chances of success before walking into that interview room. Nevertheless, we thought it would still be helpful to break down this myth and look at some scientific proof showing that it is false.

First, consider the effectiveness of training on performance and level of success. We recently conducted a study to evaluate the effectiveness of our interview preparation program for students applying for medical school. The study included 29 randomly selected students with an upcoming interview. A given student's baseline performance was the numeric score obtained from an expert's evaluation of their first realistic mock interview in BeMo's Interview Prep program. As part of the feedback for that interview, the student was coached by the expert who identified areas in need of improvement. Each student received 6 to 8 mock interviews followed by expert feedback, and the numeric scores from their final mock interviews were used to measure their improvement against the baseline. To avoid confounding factors that could interfere with our study, we used a double-blind method in which neither our students nor our experts were aware that the study was being conducted until after its completion. The results are given in Figure 2.

Effect of Expert Training on Interview Practice Scores

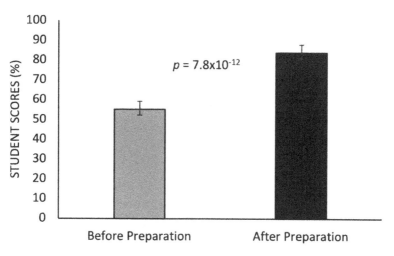

Figure 2. Applicants' interview practice scores improved by an average of 28.57% on interview simulations after 6 to 8 BeMo interview preparation sessions with expert feedback.

Before preparation, the students' average score was 55.17% (left bar). After preparation with experts, the students' average score was 83.74% (right bar). The small p-value indicates that the probability of this difference arising by chance is next to zero. Thus, we can confidently say that training works!

We additionally evaluated the effectiveness of our popular MMI Prep and CASPer Prep programs and found similar results. 44 students were included in the MMI study and their performance was evaluated after 6 to 8 sessions with mock interviews and expert feedback, while 24 students were included in the CASPer study and evaluated after only 3 sessions. The results are given in Figure 3.

Effect of Expert Training on MMI and CASPer Practice Scores

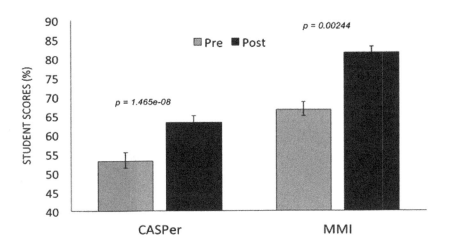

Figure 3. Applicants' MMI practice scores improved by 27% on average after 6 to 8 MMI preparation sessions and expert feedback with BeMo.

Figure 3 clearly shows a marked improvement in scores for both groups of students after training – 23% for those training for the CASPer test and 27% for those training for MMIs. When competing with thousands of other applicants, even a 1 to 2% increase in your interview score could set you apart, so an increase of more than 20% would almost certainly guarantee you an acceptance letter! Indeed, our interview preparation programs like those we tested in the studies above have an overall success rate of 93.5%, meaning that the vast majority of students who go through our programs gain acceptance into medical school and residency programs. Therefore, we firmly believe in the power of practice! Myth busted.

Of course, there are also studies supporting the opposing view that interview preparation has no effect on performance. This is likely due to a fundamental difference in what we consider as practice. Studies that find no difference in performance often equate practice with reading over and trying sample questions without any feedback. Well, we absolutely agree that this kind of preparation will not improve your interview performance! At BeMo, we have always said that practice does not make perfect, practice makes permanent. It is only *perfect* practice that makes perfect. That means you only get better at interviewing if you practice using realistic simulations followed by expert feedback. You need an interview coach to tell you what you are doing well, what you are doing poorly, and how to do better. Ideally, you would receive this kind of expert feedback throughout your interview preparation to keep you on track and make sure you are actually improving. That is the BeMo difference! Now, it is up to you how you want to move forward. You can choose to believe those myths and do nothing to prepare for your imminent residency interview, or you can reject these falsities and get to work before it's too late! We hope you have chosen the latter because we are eager continue sharing what we know with you to help you succeed. In the next chapter, we will be discussing the most common mistakes applicants make on their interviews to help you avoid making the same errors.

CHAPTER IV

5 Common Errors Made in Residency Interviews

Now that we have debunked the myths about interview preparation, let's take a look at the common mistakes applicants make when they prepare for their interviews and during the interview itself. It is important that you understand why these errors may hurt your performance and what you can do to avoid making them yourself.

In this chapter, we focus on 5 errors: lack of preparation, poor delivery, lack of structure, red flags, and inappropriate attire. As we discuss each one, evaluate your own interview practice thus far and think about whether you have made these mistakes yourself.

1. Lack of Preparation

As we have hopefully convinced you, preparation can definitely improve your interview performance. Yet, applicants still often neglect to prepare sufficiently in advance. This mistake is commonly made by those who feel confident about their interview skills, whether this confidence is well-grounded or not. It is also made by individuals with many interview invitations as they tend to become overly confident about their chances of being matched, forgetting that they still need to perform well at each interview.

As we have established in *Chapter II: Admissions Statistics and Why You Must ACE Your Residency Interview*, the interview is an extremely important part of the application process. Think of your interview as a behavioral test. It takes a long time to develop new habits and curb undesirable behaviors. Additionally, each interview you participate in will differ in content and perhaps also style. Thus, preparing for each individual interview in advance is absolutely necessary. In our experience, it takes at least 6 to 8 weeks to fully prepare for a residency interview.

Interviewers value, among other things, your interest in their particular program. One way to demonstrate this is through *preparedness*, which will be apparent if your responses are targeted, thoughtful, and well-articulated. With that in mind, research each individual program you will be interviewing for. Your ability to connect with their mission and values may make a lasting impression on the interviewers, further increasing your chances of being matched.

See Point 3 below for how to structure your interview preparation to make the most effective use of your time.

2. Poor Delivery

Confident, smooth, and well-articulated speech makes a great impression on the interviewer regardless of the content. We are not underestimating the importance of your answer contents, but the truth is that a lot of what admissions committees look at is delivery. You can have a wonderful argument to make, but if it is interrupted with pauses, filler words, or repetition, your interviewer will barely take notice of what you are saying.

It is therefore important to deliver your structured answers confidently and concisely. Interviewers seek applicants who are both eloquent and informative in their responses. It will help the interviewer follow your thought process and better understand your logic. By delivering your strong arguments in a structured way, you will not only win the case, but also leave a lasting impression on the interviewer. The following are some aspects to consider with regards to delivery.

Introductions & Conclusions

A common mistake observed among applicants is that they do not even acknowledge the interviewer at the beginning or end of their interview. However, the way you introduce yourself and say goodbye will also play a significant role in how the interviewer views you as an applicant. The introduction is the first time the interviewer gets to know you and your professional etiquette. A polite, professional greeting and introduction go a long way in making that initial positive impression on the interviewer. Therefore, it is absolutely crucial to address the interviewer with their name and professional title at the beginning of your interview and also after it has been completed.

Another common mistake is that the applicants tend to spend a long time introducing themselves and talking about their stories before the interview even begins. Although the introduction is very important, it should be concise and to-the-point.

The following is an example of a proper introduction:

Applicant: Good morning, I'm John. Who do I have the pleasure of speaking to today? (Once the interviewer has stated his/her name, acknowledge him/her by name.) Dr. Johnson, it is a pleasure to meet you. Thank you for the opportunity to interview for your program.

The following is an example of a proper conclusion:

Applicant: Thank you, Dr. Johnson, for the time spent with me today. It was a pleasure to meet you and discuss my answers with you today. Once again, I would like to express my interest in this program, and I hope to see you in the future.

Filler Words

Another commonly observed mistake during interviews is the excessive use of filler words and pauses. Each individual may use a slightly different set of filler words, but some common ones include "um", "uh", and "like". The use of filler words is habitual for some people, while for others it could be induced by contextual factors like added stress, lack of preparation, and poor vocabulary on a given topic. Some filler words can be eliminated relatively quickly, but others may require more time. Regardless, reducing the number of filler words and pauses requires great initiative and self-awareness. Have your speech evaluated by a professional interviewer or at least someone who can point out which filler words you are using and when you tend to use them. The next step is to practice. You can record yourself and self-monitor your speech, or practice with a friend or family member and ask them to restart the conversation every time you use a filler word unnecessarily. This will make you more cognizant of your mistakes and help you to minimize your use of filler words and/or pauses gradually.

Lack of Enthusiasm

Applicants often underestimate the importance of showing enthusiasm for the program they are interviewing for. They may arrive late at the interview site, show obvious signs of fatigue, and have an uncaring attitude. However, it is important to show enthusiasm from beginning to end during your interview. Arrive on-time. Create a positive atmosphere during the introduction as this will enable you to open up further and fully demonstrate your personality. Otherwise, the interviewer will be less likely to engage with you and will only have a dry conversation with you that will not set you apart from other candidates. Your level of enthusiasm can also determine whether the interviewer believes you will fit into their particular program or specialty and whether you reflect their mission statement. The interviewers will remember you by the way you carry and present yourself during that specific interaction. Remember to smile and express excitement about being there to communicate to them that their program is your number-one choice. As discussed above, it is also important to show appreciation for the people who interview you, so be sure to thank them for their time. The enthusiasm and professionalism you demonstrate during your interview go a long way to show that you care about the opportunity.

3. Lack of Structure

As previously discussed, the ability to interview well is acquired, not inherited. As part of this skill, you must learn to structure your answers so that your ideas come through the way you intended. As important as it is for you to express your point of view, it is also crucial for you to show your analytical skills and objectivity when tackling each issue. The general rule of thumb is to refrain from jumping to conclusions and lay out your arguments before presenting your opinions and proposing solutions. You do not want to come off as judgmental or biased as a result of poor structure. Of course, being able to progress through your ideas logically will also help the interviewer follow your answer and understand your points. The specific structures and strategies to use for different question types will be covered in detail in *Chapter VII: Proven Strategies to Approach and Ace 6 Common Types of Residency Interview Questions*.

Structure is not only important in your answers, but also in your preparation. In order to prepare for the most important interview in your professional career thus far, you will spend hours going over sample questions and scenarios. However, many applicants do not set out with clear objectives, are unable to identify their strengths and weaknesses, and therefore are unable to formulate a plan of action and monitor their own progress. To approach the task more systematically, have a third party evaluate your responses at different points in your preparation, and practice based on the feedback you get. If that third party is a well-trained expert, they will also be able to point out when you are not directly addressing the question, or ways in which you can address the question better. You can then target the areas that need improvement, whether that be your delivery, content, or organization. This is how you will make the best use of the time you dedicate to interview preparation and ensure that you are making good progress toward your interview goals. Also try to practice with people you don't know well so your approach to the questions is more professional and less colloquial. Introducing uncertainty to the process is extremely important during preparation as it pushes you to deliver your answers under stress, mimicking the actual interview.

Using a structured, step-by-step approach during practice will raise your confidence level, increase your vocabulary, and improve your overall delivery. Of course, there will be times where the interviewers will still surprise you with questions you were not expecting, but the previous preparation you have done will help you remain calm and think on your feet.

4. Red Flags

Among the many mistakes you could make, only 'red flags' are truly detrimental to your application score. Therefore, it is crucial for you to avoid any potential red flags during the entire application process, including at your interview. Below, we will take a look at three major red flags: dishonesty about your application or experiences, lack of ethical judgment, and unprofessional appearance.

A common red flag is when applicants present answers that are inconsistent with their application documents. Whether the applicant listed an experience just to pad their CV, or they gave an inaccurate description of their level of involvement, this lack of transparency can and will negatively influence their chances of acceptance. All programs seek and respect applicants who are, first and foremost, honest. Therefore, while you prepare for your interview, ensure that your answers are not only well-structured, but also a true reflection of you and your experiences.

Another red flag is the lack of ethical judgment. This could happen if you omit or misidentify the pressing issue in an interview scenario, which could lead you to make a poor ethical judgment in your answer. It is important to correctly identify the most pressing concern in any situation, show that you are non-judgmental and considerate of others' perspectives, not just your own. In this way, you can demonstrate to the interviewers that you are able to respond ethically in difficult situations in your future profession.

The third red flag is inappropriate attire. Since this is considered a significant red flag, it will be discussed as a separate point below.

5. Inappropriate Attire or Appearance

Professional attire and presentation during interviews are often underemphasized, but having a professional appearance goes hand-in-hand with being professional in speech. When either of these is lacking, you paint yourself as an unprepared and potentially disrespectful applicant, one that the interviewers will find difficult to value. Therefore, professional attire and appearance will be important elements to your success. Remember that medicine is still a conservative profession. You want to stand out because of your personality and outstanding communication and argumentative skills, not because of your attire. For detailed guidance on how to dress appropriately, see *Chapter IX: What to Wear, What to Say, and How to Communicate Non-verbally during Your Interview.*

Now that we have discussed the most common errors applicants make during their interviews and how you can avoid them, we can begin to discuss the residency interview itself. This will be the contents of the next few chapters. We begin in the next chapter with the types of interviews you may encounter and the proven strategies to help you ace them.

CHAPTER V

Different Types of Residency Interviews

A s you may recall that in the first chapter, we discussed how interviews have evolved. One thing to note is that interview formats continue to develop, and though programs often use one particular format, they could also change it each year. For this reason, it is important for you to become familiar with all interview formats. This chapter breaks down the types of interviews you may encounter on your application journey to give you a good understanding of their structure, why each is used, who you will be interviewed by, and what these interviewers are looking for. At various points throughout this chapter, we mention question types that are common in each of these interview formats. These will be defined and discussed in detail in *Chapter VII: Proven Strategies to Approach and Ace 6 Common Types of Residency Interview Questions*.

In any type of interview, the following three components will be factored into your score:

Content:

What you say is obviously crucial! You will likely be evaluated on the validity of your ideas, the strength of your arguments and examples, the lessons you propose to have learned from your personal experiences, the justifications for actions you propose to take, and so forth.

Delivery:

Of course, interviewers will also consider how well you communicate the content of your answer. They want to see that you can present your points in an organized and concise way, without rambling or going on tangents, and with minimal filler words. As a resident, you will have to relay complex information to patients and colleagues in a way that can be easily understood. Therefore, delivery in both verbal and written communication is key!

Suitability for the profession:

Based on what you say and how you say it, the interviewers will make a judgment on how well-suited you are for both the profession of medicine and also their particular program. Have you demonstrated that you are a mature and thoughtful individual who works well with others? Did you show leadership and advocacy skills? Do your values align with those of the program? Educate yourself before your interview by doing thorough research. You will then know what types of qualities they are looking for.

1. Traditional Interviews: One-on-One

What is a traditional one-on-one interview?

In a traditional one-on-one interview, a single candidate is interviewed by one interviewer. Your program may have just one traditional interview, or it could have two or three one-on-one interviews where you move from room to room. During your interview, you will be asked a series of questions and the interviewer will give their overall impression of your performance to the admissions committee.

Traditional interviews tend to be short, lasting 20 minutes on average. This means you must practice making your answers in-depth, yet concise!

Your interview can be *open-* or *closed-*file. An open interview means the interviewers have seen some or all of your application documents, including your transcript, personal statement, and reference letters, and are free to ask you about anything on your application during the interview. If you are told your interview will be open, or if it is not explicitly stated which type of interview it will be, you should review your application documents in detail prior to the interview to prepare for questions that pertain to the experiences you discussed therein. In contrast, a closed interview means the interviewers know nothing about you but your name. The questions you are asked in this interview will therefore not be tailored to your profile. However, the interviewers may still ask you to elaborate on the experiences and ideas you bring up in your answers to previous questions, so you should be prepared to discuss them in more detail.

Most traditional interviews will focus on asking personal or program-based questions about your past experiences, why you are pursuing medicine, and why you are interested in their program. However, they can still ask for your views about current issues, give you scenarios to respond to, or anything else! You must therefore be prepared to answer any type of question at your interview.

A traditional interview is usually not rigidly structured. If the interviewers have prepared questions, you can expect between 7 to 10 questions. Otherwise, the interview may be conversational, and the interviewer will follow your lead and see where the conversation goes before deciding which questions to ask you. For this reason, a traditional interview may not have a strict scoring rubric or a scoring sheet. The interviewer may be asked to simply share their thoughts about you with the admissions committee after your interview.

Who are your interviewers?

A traditional interview is typically conducted by a representative of the medical school faculty in the specialty you have applied to or current residents.

Why is this format used?

Traditional interviews are still used because they are inexpensive, straightforward, and flexible. Being less structured, it is far easier for the interviewers to follow up on any points you make that need clarification or address potential red flags in your CV or your answers. Interviewers are typically friendly and collegial, and hence can put the candidate at ease and get them to open up about their story and experiences.

2. Traditional Interviews: Panel

What is a traditional panel?

This is the most common type of interview conducted for residency. A panel interview is one that is conducted with anywhere from 2 to 5 interviewers (occasionally more) in one room at the same time. The length of a panel interview ranges from program to program but is typically 20 to 45 minutes.

Similar to one-on-one interviews, these can be open or closed, and can include a variety of questions from personal to situational types. We will go into these types and others in the next chapter.

Who are your interviewers?

Similar to traditional one-on-one interviews, the interviewers will consist of faculty members and current residents. Since there are multiple interviewers, one of them may also be a community representative or an allied health professional. The community member may be there to assess how well you communicate with someone who has no medical background.

Why is this format used?

Panel style tends to be used because they allow the interviewers to take a more collaborative and thorough approach. Each interviewer can ask follow-up questions to address points other panelists may have missed, and importantly, it allows for multiple assessments of the same candidate in their interactions with different interviewers, therefore making the process more objective.

3. Multiple Mini Interviews (MMI)

What is the MMI?

The famous and much-feared Multiple Mini Interview, or MMI, was developed at McMaster University and has slowly spread to medical schools and other professional programs throughout the world.

Unlike traditional interviews, where the same interviewer or panel asks all the questions, an MMI consists of 8 to 12 stations, each with a different interviewer. At each station, you, the candidate, have 1.5 to 2 minutes to read and think about the question outside the room, and 4 to 8 minutes inside the room to respond to the prompt as well as any follow-up questions the interviewer may have. Once this time is up, you move to the next station, and the cycle repeats until you have cycled through all the stations.

All MMIs are necessarily closed interviews with a standard scoring protocol. The interviewer at each station will score you on a scale of 1 (poor) to 10 (outstanding) based on a) the strength of your arguments and content, b) your communication skills and the delivery of your answer, and c) your suitability for the profession of medicine. Note that your score for a given station is *relative* to that of other candidates for the same station. Thus, you can still get a relatively high score at a station that you found difficult if it was difficult for everyone.

Although scenario or situational type questions are commonly asked on MMIs, you can expect to be asked any question type at an MMI station, so be prepared for all possible question types.

Who are your interviewers?

MMI assessors are a mix of faculty members, current residents, and community members or allied health professionals. Each assessor will be sitting at one station and score all 8 to12 candidates who come through that station in a given cycle.

Keep in mind that MMI assessors are trained not to give any positive or negative feedback to candidates. They may have minimal interaction with you during your station and may simply sit and look at you, without smiling or acknowledging your thoughts. They are instructed to not give any sort of feedback, either through their expressions or words, as they are aiming to not influence your answer in any way. Do not be thrown off by this or feel as if your answer is not strong because the interviewer is expressionless. This is normal for the MMI!

Why is this format used?

MMIs allow programs to interview a large number of applicants in a much shorter period of time, making it a more efficient process. The interviewers also know nothing about you, which may eliminate some of the bias inherent in open interviews where they may be aware of your grades or which medical school you attended. You will receive independent scores from at least 8 people, which means doing poorly at one station need not affect your score at the next station, and you can still do very well overall. This scoring method can also remove the candidate ordering bias that is of concern in other interview formats. Since candidates rotate through the stations and no one is always first or always last, any biases the interviewers have when scoring earlier vs. later candidates is cancelled out when the scores are pooled.

Although it is impossible to completely eliminate human biases in the interview process, the promise of a more objective and efficient way of interviewing applicants has made the MMI the interview format of choice for many medical schools worldwide.

For more information on the MMI, including research about its validity and reliability, we refer you to our book *BeMo's Ultimate Guide to the Multiple Mini Interview (MMI)*.

4. Hybrid Interviews

What is a hybrid interview?

A hybrid interview is one that combines elements of both a traditional interview and an MMI. Typically, this will consist of an MMI with fewer stations, preceded or followed by one or more traditional one-on-one or panel interviews. For example, you may have a 5-station MMI, followed by a 10-minute panel interview with two panelists. The format and scoring protocols of each portion of the interview should follow what we have outlined above. Keep in mind that while the MMI portion will always be closed, the traditional interview can be closed or open.

Who are your interviewers?

You will have the same mix of interviewers mentioned above: faculty members, current residents, and community members.

Why is this format used?

Quite simply, some programs want the combined benefits of both interview formats. They want to have the promised objectivity of the MMI alongside the more collegial and personal traditional interview in the hopes of getting a fuller picture of each applicant.

5. Virtual or Video Interview

What is a virtual or video interview?

More recently, some universities have opted for an online, virtual or video interview. In this interview format, there are no live interviewers; candidates simply record themselves responding to pre-prepared question prompts. The number of questions, type of questions used, and how much time you have to respond to each are program-specific. However, the logistics remain fairly consistent. Usually, you would receive instructions and login details to an online interviewing platform from the school. While some schools allow you to schedule your own interview within a given timeframe, others would simply assign you a time slot or give you a timeframe to submit your responses. Since technical problems are common, some schools also allow you to practice using their online platform before doing the real interview. Once all the responses have been recorded and uploaded, they are sent to the reviewers for scoring. It may be the case that all the responses of an applicant are reviewed by the same person or group of people. However, it is more likely that each response is independently evaluated by a different person, much like the MMI.

Who are your interviewers?

There are no live interviewers, but the group of people scoring these video responses will be comprised of faculty members, current residents, and other members of the admissions committee, such as allied professionals. On this aspect, virtual interviews are not different from live interviews.

Why is this format used?

Such interviews are utilized for a number of reasons, some to do with efficiency, and others to do with eliminating bias. First, this interview format can drastically speed up the interview process since a large number of interviews can be conducted simultaneously, and responses from all applicants can be collected within a fairly short period of time. From the candidate's perspective, this interview format allows them to participate in the interview from the comfort of their own home. More importantly, it saves them the time and cost of travelling to an interview site, thus removing some potential barriers that make on-site interviews difficult or even impossible for some individuals. Furthermore, candidates' responses cannot be influenced by feedback, verbal or non-verbal, from an interviewer, so virtual interviews can also be effective in eliminating interviewer biases.

We hope that this breakdown of the interview formats has given you some insight into how to prepare for your own interview. In the next chapter, we will go through a number of proven strategies to help you in this process!

CHAPTER VI

Pre-mortem: 18 Proven Strategies to Prepare for and Ace Any Residency Interview

As emphasized in previous chapters, you *can* and absolutely *must* prepare for residency interviews in advance. All human behavior is learned, and just like for any exam, there are specific strategies you can use to ace your interview. This chapter will provide you with an overview of the general interviewing strategies we teach students in our sought-after residency interview preparation programs. We know from experience that they work, and they work consistently. Therefore, take the time to read this chapter multiple times before you move on, and keep referring to these instructions as you prepare for your actual interview. Many of them will be expanded in later chapters.

What to do during any interview:

1. Think like the interviewers.

Recall that in the previous chapter, we shared the 3 main aspects you will be scored on in any interview format. These are the following:

a) Communication skills (how well you delivered your answer)
b) Content (your ideas and arguments)
c) Your suitability for the medical profession and for the specific program

In order to think like the interviewer, imagine you are on the other side of the process and you are given a scoring sheet. For each response you give, ask yourself how well it measures on each of these aspects and how you might adjust your response to achieve a better score. One of the many things we encourage our students to do in our interview preparation programs is to reflect on their own performance, evaluate themselves, and monitor their own progress in between sessions. We even ask them to create new sample questions to answer, which helps them understand and internalize what interviewers are looking for. In order to do well in an interview, it is important to be acutely aware of the criteria on which your evaluation will be based.

2. Learn to manage your stress.

One of the most common reasons applicants do poorly on their interviews is their inability to control their stress level. Nothing is worse than feeling so nervous that you are unable to formulate a coherent response. Among other things, poor delivery would certainly have a negative impact on the interviewer's evaluation of your communication skills. Remember also that medicine is a stressful profession, and interviewers need to see that you can manage it well.

This point is so important that we have dedicated an entire chapter to long-term and short-term strategies for stress management. Read *Chapter X: How to Manage Stress* to learn more!

3. Think before responding/Read each prompt at least twice.

Candidates often feel as though they must begin answering the prompt as soon as they enter the MMI station or as soon as the interviewer finishes asking the question. This is never the case! Make sure you take your time to read and/or think over each question at least *twice* before answering.

For an MMI, you will have time outside the room to gather your thoughts and organize your answer. Since, in practice, an organized and concise response should take no longer than 3 to 4 minutes to execute, you might be able to afford an extra minute or two outside the room to make sure you understand the question even after the buzzer sounds. If you do enter the room late, make sure you briefly apologize for the delay, and explain that you wanted a bit more time to gather your thoughts before delivering your response. This will actually put you ahead of your competition because it shows your ability to think carefully and deliberate, even in high-stress situations.

If your question is given to you verbally, as would be the case in a traditional interview, it would be perfectly acceptable to say, "May I please have a moment to organize my thoughts?" Then, take the time to think about what you want to say and how you want to say it. If you rush, you are more likely to miss key information, your answer will be less organized, and you may even give a biased response.

4. Use the *primacy effect* to your advantage.

It goes without saying that once you enter the room, you must smile, greet the interviewer by name, introduce yourself, and when appropriate, shake hands – all before delivering your response. This is something candidates often miss because they are too nervous to remember that the interview is also a test of their professionalism. Interestingly, your interviewer is more likely to remember the first moments of your interaction compared to everything that follows. This is a well-documented phenomenon in psychology called the *primacy effect*, which is the tendency for people to recall earlier events better than later events. Thus, when you are being evaluated, nuances at the beginning of your interview can make a significant difference!

5. Master your non-verbal communication skills.

There is ample evidence in the literature that non-verbal cues make up for a large portion of human communication compared to verbal communication. This includes using eye contact, facial expressions, and posture.

Eye contact:

We are hardwired to look into other people's eyes because they are an important mode of communication. For example, infants, who are unable to talk, are able to communicate with their parents with something as simple as eye contact. This is why you may have seen a crying infant going into an almost instant calm after making eye contact with his or her mother. During your interview, maintain eye contact about 70% of the time to communicate confidence to the interviewers. This also shows that you are being respectful and paying close attention. Remember not to stare intently, as this can create a tense atmosphere and make the interviewer feel uncomfortable. If maintaining eye contact does not come naturally to you, practice!

Facial expressions:

Humans are hard-wired to detect happiness, sadness, fear, surprise, disgust, anger, and so forth simply by reading the micro-expressions on each other's faces. Your goal, as an interviewee, is to communicate specific emotions at appropriate moments. When you enter the interview room, for example, you need to show that you are excited and happy to be there, even though you might actually feel anxious at first. Your facial expression should differ when you are sharing a positive experience versus a negative one, and when you are discussing a vulnerable party versus a party with malicious intent. If you are in an MMI acting station and the actor reveals that they just received news of their mother's passing, you must reflect their sorrow and show genuine concern. For any hypothetical situation, try to immerse yourself in the scenario as much as possible and respond as you would if it were actually happening. That way, the emotions you bring and the facial expressions that come with them will be genuine.

Genuine smile:

There is a difference between a fake smile and a genuine smile. A genuine smile induces wrinkles around the eyes, whereas a fake one does not, and humans are exceptionally good at distinguishing the two at a subconscious level. If your smile is fake, you appear untrustworthy to the interviewer, but if you smile with your mouth and your eyes, you convey the kind of charisma and emotional generosity that draws people in and makes you stand out in their memories. Rather than putting on a fake 'genuine smile', think about the positive aspects of your interview, the prospect of being matched, or any other happy thoughts that would help you bring a genuine smile to your interview.

Body posture:

Your body language says a lot about you, without you ever saying a word. When you are interacting with someone, whether it be an interviewer, an actor, or another applicant, make sure you are standing in front of them at a slight angle. Standing behind someone can increase their anxiety because they cannot anticipate what you are going to do if they cannot see you, but standing directly in front of them may be interpreted as confrontational. Make sure you are standing or sitting at an appropriate distance from others. If you are too close, it may seem intimidating and you may be invading their space, but if you are too far, you may seem too distant, aloof, or cold. Also be aware of what you are doing with your hands and arms. Standing with your hands on your hips can convey aggression and crossing your arms signifies defensiveness or insecurity. If you are sitting down while listening to someone, lean slightly forward to show focus and interest.

If you found these helpful, stay tuned for *Chapter IX: What to Wear, What to Say, and How to Communicate Non-verbally during Your Interview* where we will address more points about non-verbal communication!

6. Identify the most pressing issue.

Your first task after reading or hearing an interview question is to figure out the most pressing issue. Generally, this is the wellbeing of those under your care or of a vulnerable group such as patients, students, children, and so forth. You must ask yourself whether someone's safety is at stake or if there are larger implications for society as a whole. If you are a doctor, your primary concern is for the wellbeing of your patients. If you are a teacher, it is the wellbeing of your students. If you are the captain of an oil tanker, and the tanker is leaking, the most pressing issue is the wellbeing of your crew and the immediate and long-term impact of an oil leak on the environment. Many scenarios will include distracting information or multiple perspectives. If there are multiple issues or multiple vulnerable parties, if may even be necessary for you to prioritize one or some over others after you have identified them. Identifying the pressing issue is especially important for scenario questions, but it may be useful for policy-related questions as well. Moreover, your ability to quickly and accurately identify the pressing issue comes with practice.

7. Always remain non-judgmental.

Whether you are exploring a controversial issue or discussing how you would handle a situation involving the wrong-doing or ignorance of others, you must remain non-judgmental. For questions about controversial issues, do not prematurely dismiss the reasoning and arguments from either side. Explore both sides of the argument without bias, and only state your own views after weighing both pros and cons. For scenario questions, do not assume that the other party is aware of their actions, has control over what they did, or has malintent. If you are in a position of power, do not assume that the other individual knows less than you or that you are necessarily right. A professional always reserves judgment and holds off on acting until they have fully assessed the situation.

8. Gather all the facts. Don't make any assumptions.

Interview questions are often intentionally missing key information. The interviewers are interested to see if you are going to identify what is missing and gather all the facts first or make a hasty judgment of the situation and respond inappropriately. Let's assume in an acting question, the actor playing your friend, Tony, tells you that a man who might be intoxicated is walking to his car to drive away. You might be inclined to react by stopping the man immediately. However, it is important to take a step back and gather information by asking the right questions. Why does Tony think the man is intoxicated? If it's because he smelled alcohol in the man's breath as he walked past, how do we know it isn't because he's diabetic and what Tony smelled was ketoacidosis? What if the man is indeed drunk, but he is simply going to grab something from his car? You simply don't know until you gather all the facts.

Keep in mind, if gathering facts involves discussing a sensitive topic with another individual, you must explicitly mention it will be a *private* conversation. As a professional, you never want to embarrass the person in front of others unless it is absolutely unavoidable. If you are describing your approach rather than acting it out, you may also want to make clear to the interviewer that you are approaching the conversation calmly, in a non-confrontational manner, and that you would want to maintain a neutral, friendly tone to avoid escalating the situation. If you do not make this clear, the interviewer will be free to assume your demeanor however they deem appropriate. That is too significant a factor to leave unaddressed when your communication skills are being evaluated. Just as you don't want to make assumptions in your response, you also don't want to give the interviewer room to make assumptions about your behavior in a delicate situation.

9. Determine who is directly or indirectly involved.

As a professional, you need to understand that real-life situations impact not only those directly involved in the situation, but also others on the periphery. Let's say you are about to fire the assistant coach of your college basketball team for professional misconduct. You, the coach, and the rest of the team are directly involved, but the college, the college basketball community, and the coach's family will also be impacted by your actions. Demonstrating awareness of the complexities of real-life situations and the repercussions of your actions in the world indicates a high level of professionalism and maturity.

10. Learn to identify the type of question and have a strategy for each.

It is impossible for you to predict the exact interview questions you may encounter, but if you learn to identify the different question *types* and common *themes* and have a strategy for each, you will have a better chance of acing them during your interview. We will identify these question types and go through strategies to answer them in the next chapter, so review them before and during practice!

11. Familiarize yourself with professional ethics.

You will inevitably encounter interview questions that touch on professional ethics. For physicians, this includes topics like informed consent, patient autonomy, confidentiality, and professional boundaries, amongst others. Therefore, it would be beneficial for you to read some *general* books about professional ethics in the field of medicine. We don't have specific recommendations, but a Google or Amazon search should give you plenty of options, as can your university or college library.

12. Provide the most rational and common-sense solution that causes the least amount of harm to those involved.

Having said the above, applicants often spend a considerable amount of time reading advance medical ethics books, but that is not necessary and often leads to frustration. You do not need to be an ethicist to do well on questions that touch on these issues. To show professionalism, all you need to do is demonstrate that you can make common sense decisions and come up with rational responses that cause as little harm to others as possible.

13. Get comfortable with awkward silences.

In timed interviews like the MMI, candidates often feel the need to keep talking until they run out of time or get cut off, instead of bringing their response to a firm conclusion. As a result, they compromise the quality of their answer for unnecessary quantity and end up displaying poor communication and time management skills. Remember, this is a test of your communication skills more than anything else. When you are being concise and your response is effective, you are likely to complete your answer before the time is up. If the interviewer does not have any follow-up questions, you need to be comfortable with the silence that will ensue until the buzzer sounds.

14. Don't forget to say your goodbyes!

Remember when we talked about the primacy effect earlier? Your second-best friend during your interview is the *recency effect*. This is another well-documented principle in psychology, dictating that people remember the last piece of information presented to them in more detail than what was said earlier in a conversation. Therefore, it is critical that you give a positive impression before leaving your interview. It's not rocket science; simply smile, thank the interviewer for their time, and politely say goodbye before exiting the room.

15. Dedicate at least 6 to 8 weeks to prepare for the interview.

Think of your interview as a behavioral test. Just like for any other test, you must start preparing well in advance because it takes a long time to develop new habits and curb undesirable behaviors. In our experience, it takes at least 6 to 8 weeks to fully prepare for a residency interview.

16. Avoid overreliance on books and guides.

Books, like this one, are a good starting point for interview preparation, but once you have understood the background knowledge, it will be time to put theory into practice, which brings us to the next point.

17. Practice using realistic mock interviews.

Just like any other functional skill, the only way to improve your interview performance is to deliberately and repeatedly engage in the task. Reading interviews guides and sample questions is insufficient unless it is coupled with realistic practice. This can be achieved with simulations and mock interviews, which are effective in removing the 'fear of the unknown' and making you less nervous and more confident on the day of your interview.

18. Remember that PERFECT practice makes perfect.

Lastly, only *perfect* practice makes perfect. If you are practicing with ineffective strategies, you are going to form bad habits, which become difficult to correct and may impede your interview performance. Therefore, after you practice in simulations or mock interviews, it is crucial that you get feedback. This feedback should come from an *expert* such as a practicing health care professional, university professor, or a trained expert, *not* a friend or family member. Only an expert will be able to give you a professional, objective assessment of your interview performance and recommendations on how to improve. This is the most effective way to prepare for your interview. Period.

When you enroll in one of BeMo's prep programs, you will get access to realistic mock interviews followed by one-on-one expert feedback. The expert will over each of your responses, identify your strengths and weaknesses, and give you strategies on how to do better next time. We will continue to work with you until you are confident about your upcoming interview. To learn more, visit our website at BeMoResidencyInterview.com

Free Goodwill

A message from our CEO, Behrouz Moemeni

My mentor always used to say, "Behrouz, you should give until it hurts." What he meant by this is giving your time and resources to those who are less fortunate or experienced than you to empower them to get to the next level on their journey, whatever that may be. People who lend a hand to others with zero expectations for return experience higher life satisfaction and self-fulfillment and are generally more successful in their careers. However, I have learned that supporting others can be a lot simpler than what you may think. You don't have to spend a lot of time or money, and it doesn't actually have to "hurt" to help. It starts with the simple things and grows as you gain the resources to do more.

As you probably know, I created BeMo to provide as much information as possible to everyone. I think information should be available to all for little to no cost. That's why, at BeMo, we create books, videos, extensive blogs, and other resources at little to no cost to students, even though they cost us a lot to create. We only charge for our private consulting and preparation programs, and even then, the value we create for our students is infinitely more than the cost of our services. For example, think of the lifetime value of becoming a medical doctor, dentist, and so forth (e.g., by doing some quick math and multiplying only 20 years of work at an average of $250,000/year salary). Though the return on investment is crystal clear, we want students to start with a low-cost commitment to see the benefit first; we want students to choose us to be their private mentors only if they find value in our work and commit only when they are ready to invest in themselves, which we facilitate with interest-free installment plans. This is why we provide all the information necessary for anyone to do this on their own, if they choose to do so. However, the only way for us, at BeMo, to accomplish our audacious mission of helping one billion students is by reaching as many people as possible.

So, I'd like to create an opportunity for you to help others you don't know with a few minutes of your time. Think of those who will go through the same journey as you in the future. They are less experienced, have less resources, and maybe have no idea where to start. If you have found the information in this book valuable so far, would you please write us a quick review on Amazon?

Most people judge a book like this by its cover and its reviews. Your review will help someone...

get to the next level...

advance in their career...

achieve life fulfillment...

and...*help others.*

It will take you less than 60 seconds to make all of this happen...please leave a review on Amazon.

Thank you very much from the bottom of my heart for helping us with our mission.

To your success,

Behrouz Moemeni, Ph.D.

CEO @ BeMo

CHAPTER VII

Proven Strategies to Approach and Ace 6 Common Types of Residency Interview Questions

While you cannot predict the exact questions you will be asked, you can certainly prepare for the *types* of questions you will encounter. Once you are familiar with the question types, you can formulate a strategy for each of them. This will ensure that, no matter what they ask you on the day of your interview, you will be able to give a well-organized, in-depth, and concise answer.

As we outline the different question types and suggest strategies for tackling each, you may be tempted to skip over a few, especially if you have heard that some question types were not used by a particular program in a previous cycle. Indeed, depending on the program and interview style they choose, you will be more likely to encounter some question types than others. However, keep in mind that each program can change their interview format or the question types from one year to the next without any prior notice to applicants. Therefore, the best strategy is to make sure you are ready for every type of question, regardless of the historical trends for a specific school. The last thing you want on your interview day is to be bamboozled by questions you have not prepared for in advance when you had a chance to do so. Of course, it is also possible that you see a brand-new question type that is not discussed in this book. That is totally normal and it means that the question is likely a new test question. Our goal in this book is not to go over all possible types of questions, but rather to teach you the most common types of questions. If you know how to successfully answer at least 80% of them, you are going to be in the 90th percentile of all your peers, which is sufficient to help you become a successful applicant and a better individual.

The 6 categories of question types we will look at in this chapter are:

1. Personal Questions

2. Program-Specific Questions

3. MMI-Type Questions (Please note: Although these question types are common on MMIs, they can show up in *any* interview format. The other question types can also show up in MMIs.)

   a. Scenario- or situation-based

   b. Acting

   c. Picture-based

   d. Video-based

   e. Writing sample

4. Policy-based or Hot Topics Questions

5. Quirky Questions

6. Collaborative or Task-Based Questions

For each question type, we will outline its characteristics and strategies for answering it.

1. Personal Questions

Personal questions are designed for the interviewer to get to know more about you and your life experiences. These types of questions, like interviews, can be characterized as *closed* (not based on any knowledge of your application) or *open* (based on at least some of the details in your application, including your grades, test scores, personal statement, CV, or reference letters).

Personal questions are sometimes open-ended, for example, "Tell me about yourself." or "Why have you decided on this specialty?". They can also be used to probe you about specific positive or negative experiences you have had. Examples of positive and negative questions are "What would you say is your greatest accomplishment?" and "Describe a time you had a conflict with a superior.", respectively. You may also be asked about the experiences on your application documents if you have an open interview, such as "Tell us more about your hospital volunteering experience.". Alternatively, the interviewer may choose to ask you about the behavioral traits or skills you gained from your experiences, rather than about the experiences themselves, for example, "What is your approach to resolving conflicts?".

1. Open-ended personal questions

Open-ended personal questions tend to be the most challenging because you must give a genuine response that concisely threads together your motivations and multiple experiences. For these questions, remember not to regurgitate *every* experience you have ever had or try to mention every single item on your CV. Rather, be selective about the points you discuss so your answer can be concise. Focus on a maximum of 3 experiences you genuinely feel you learned a lot from and include detailed, personal examples so you are *showing*, and not just *telling*, the interviewer what you learned. A good way to thread these experiences together is chronologically to ensure that your answer is easy to for the interviewer to follow. This will also make it easy for you to remember! Also be sure to link your experiences with good transitional phrases so that the interviewer can easily see the connections between them.

Crafting a concise but in-depth answer to an open-ended question is not easy. To prepare for these types of questions, you must sit down well in advance and spend time in introspection. What are three experiences that really highlight who you are as a person? What are the three biggest reasons you are pursuing this specialty and not another specialty? Take the time to reflect deeply on your personal motivations so your answers are unique to you. Jot them down on a piece of paper and think through specific experiences and details you can use as supporting evidence. Also think about how each experience relates to the other, so that you can effectively transition between them. Once you have your main points and supporting details, and you know how they are all connected, you can begin practicing your answer out loud. Taking time to self-reflect will ensure you have an outline of your answer ready to go, and you will not feel flustered when answering these challenging questions.

2. Questions about specific experiences or traits

Now, let's turn to personal questions that ask about specific experiences or behavioral traits. Consider the question "Tell us about a time you resolved a conflict." as an example. The main mistake applicants make with this type of question is to spend all of their time describing an incidence when they resolved a conflict. The goal here is to not only recount the experience, but more importantly, to tell the interviewer what you *learned* from that experience and how you hope to *apply* those lessons to resolve future conflicts, especially situations you may encounter in the profession of medicine. Yes, you should highlight the lessons learned and skills developed even if the interviewer does not ask you to do so, because this is your chance to show your maturity and ability to self-reflect, learn, and change. To begin preparing for these questions, sit down with your application documents and ask yourself what you have learned from each of the experiences you have highlighted. What skills and values did you gain that will make you a better physician? Jot these down in point form on a piece of paper, then practice answering some example questions of this type.

You may have noticed that for any question you identify as *personal*, you must *always* provide a specific personal example that relates to the question. Here are three simple steps to help you structure each example:

> *1. Describe the experience.*

Most candidates think that this is the focus of the example they give. It's not! The description of the experience should be no more than 2 to 3 sentences. The purpose of describing a specific experience is to support the lessons you propose to have learned and the skills you claim to have demonstrated with tangible evidence. If you are describing a challenging situation or obstacle, be sure to include how you acted to overcome it and highlight the positive outcome.

While being concise with the description, it is also important to go in-depth and be specific. Compare the two examples below:

> *Vague example:* While volunteering at the downtown hospital, I got the chance to meet many patients from different walks of life. Though we didn't always share the same culture, language, or education background, I was able to form meaningful relationships with them and make them feel at ease while they waited for their doctors.

> *Specific example:* While volunteering at the downtown hospital, I got the chance to meet many patients from different walks of life. One of these was a woman named Sabrina who immigrated to the U.S. from the Philippines. Though she didn't speak English and I didn't speak Tagalog, I was able to relay the attending physician's messages to her using a series of hand gestures and I continued to reassure her to make her feel at ease in the unfamiliar hospital environment.

Note that the first example and the second example are demonstrating the same interpersonal skills. However, the second is much more tangible to the interviewer because the candidate discusses a specific interaction they had with a patient rather than speaking about their experience as a whole.

2. Identify the lessons learned and/or skills exhibited.

This should be the focus of your example. Interviewers are most interested in knowing what lessons and skills you learned from your past that are transferable to your future. This helps them assess your potential and suitability for the profession and specialty. If you are discussing an observation you made, say what traits you saw in the professionals you worked with that you admire and want to emulate. If you were directly involved in the interaction you described, then explicitly outline the traits you exhibited. It may be helpful when giving an example to work backwards and identify the traits you want to discuss first, then come up with the specific experience that would best illustrate these traits. Be sure to familiarize yourself with the skills and competencies that your program and other governing bodies in medicine are after in their candidates. You can do this by researching the mission and candidate ranking criteria for each program you are interviewing at.

3. Relate those lessons and skills to your future profession.

Lastly, you can connect your skills to your future work environment to demonstrate to the interviewers that you understand how your skills can help you succeed in your future role. It is always more convincing if you can identify the specific context in which the skills or traits will become useful. Compare the following:

> *Weak application:* I hope to continue to use my strong communication skills and cultural competency to connect with patients in the future.

> *Strong application:* As someone who aspires to work with underrepresented groups in the downtown area, I know I will encounter many patients who do not share my cultural, linguistic, and educational background. However, I strongly believe that I will be able to overcome these barriers with my excellent

communication skills and cultural competency to form meaningful, lasting relationships with those I serve.

In the first application, the candidate states that their skills will be helpful in their future career but remains vague about how and when they might be used. In the second application, the candidate makes a much stronger connection between their skills and their future profession, identifying the specific patient population their skills will benefit.

2. Program-Specific Questions

When you are interviewing for residency, you are interviewing for a particular program. Therefore, you may be asked questions about that program. Every residency program has a mission statement and values they espouse, as well as particular qualities they are looking for in their residents, so the interviewer will want to ensure you are a good fit for their program.

Examples of program-specific questions are "Why would you like to attend our residency program?", "One of our core values is patient-centered care. How have you exemplified this?", and "If you could change anything about our program, what would it be?".

To answer these types of questions well, you will need to get familiar with the program, their mission statement, values, curriculum, research opportunities, and extracurricular activities or clubs available to residents. Hopefully you already did a lot of this research when you decided to apply there, but here are some questions to get you thinking as you prepare: Where is the university or hospital located and what are the demographics of the population in that area? What is the profile of the current resident cohort? Does every resident have elective experience at that program? What types of fellowships are pursued by residents? You can find this information by visiting the program website. Take the opportunity to try to do an elective during clerkship at that program, or you can even talk to someone in their admissions office or a current resident and ask questions about the program, the curriculum, and the current residents.

Once you have thoroughly done your research about the program, sit down and identify 3 unique reasons why you would like to attend that particular program and which of your experiences make you a good fit. These can be reasons relating to aspects of the curriculum, how you reflect the program's core values, how you fit into the resident body, or even what you like about the location of the program. Remember to always use your experiences as examples and discuss what you learned. If patient-centered care is valued by the program, you can talk about the skills you have garnered through your clerkship experiences. If they value research, discuss your most interesting research project and why you are committed to this area of study. If you are asked what improvements or modifications you would make to the program, identify the area that needs change and use the opportunity to say how you will *personally* make this happen. This demonstrates to the interviewer that you are proactive and willing to take responsibility. For example, if the program does not have a resident wellness program and you have volunteering experience in mental health, you may want to propose starting a program that promotes work-life balance and brings mental health resources to the resident body at that school.

Reflect on these points now so you are not coming up with them during your interview. Your answer to "Why our program?" is a way to show the interviewer that you are interested in their program.

3. MMI-Type Questions

a. Scenario- or situation-based

In scenario questions, you will be given a hypothetical role in a hypothetical situation and asked how you would approach or solve it. These types of questions are common even in traditional interviews, so the strategies you will learn have a broad application.

The question prompts are based on real-life situations and may not be related to the profession of medicine. For example, you might be asked how you would resolve a conflict between two friends, or how you would deal with a disgruntled customer in a coffee shop. As you can imagine, a scenario question can touch upon many different themes. We discuss 23 of these below.

23 Scenario Themes

1. Conflict of interest

A conflict of interest refers to any scenario in which individuals, contrary to their obligations and absolute duties to act for the benefit of those they serve, exploit their relationships or status for their own personal benefit. For example, a hospital director is in a conflict of interest if she insists on using products from a company that periodically sends her gifts. A teacher who is grading tests of his close friend's son is also in a conflict of interest.

Here are a few really interesting examples for you to think about. A university professor in charge of education research who creates a for-profit admission screening company from his publicly-funded research is said to be in a conflict of interest because he would not be able to objectively judge new advances in the field if such advances threaten the existence of his newly formed for-profit venture. A university professor who is a director of a for-profit company, such as an admissions screening company, is in a conflict of interest if she speaks publicly – for example, at an information webinar for students taking the admissions test – and introduces herself as a professor of the university instead of the director of the company. Similarly, a public university that is tasked with advancing knowledge is in a conflict of interest when its ability to advance discovery is impeded by its interests in a for-profit spin-off company. Do any of these sound familiar?

2. Ethical or moral dilemma

These are scenarios in which any decision you make will lead to the violation of some moral or ethical code. For example, let's say you are a physician in an emergency room and you simultaneously receive two patients who both need a kidney transplant to survive, but you only have one kidney available. Choosing either of the patients would harm the other. Or, you witness your best friend stealing from her abusive boss at work who has not paid your friend for the past 2 months. Reporting the unethical behavior of the boss would help your friend, but she will likely also face legal consequences for stealing. The interviewer will want to see that you can make ethically and morally sound decisions even when scenarios appear to be impossible.

3. Professional boundaries, obligations, and ethics

These types of scenarios deal with instances in which effective and appropriate interactions and relationships between the professionals and the public are violated. For instance, a professor having relations with his student outside of the academic setting would be overstepping his professional boundaries with that student.

4. Scope of practice

All professionals have a certain scope of practice. These are laws and regulations that define the procedures, actions, and processes that are permitted for a licensed professional. For example, only medical doctors can prescribe medication within their scope of practice. If any other professional prescribes medication, they are said to be acting outside of their scope of practice. Similarly, a physician who has specialized in neurology cannot advise patients on the pathologies of the kidney; they would be acting outside of their scope. Likewise, a math teacher is best suited to teach math and not genetics. We can extend this notion to the general boundaries of responsibility for non-professionals as well. For example, as a friend of a patient, you would be overstepping your boundaries by inquiring of the patient's condition from their physician. As a volunteer at a homeless shelter, you would be acting outside of your role by suggesting treatment options to those who are visiting the shelter. Though these may seem like obvious boundaries to observe, candidates often suggest solutions or courses of action that overstep them in their responses.

5. Social and current events awareness

Some scenario questions incorporate real policy issues to test your awareness of current events and news about the profession. These are questions that ask you to address an issue (e.g., indigenous health) in a specific role (e.g., as a member of the indigenous community, a health care professional, or a policy maker). These types of questions demand you to navigate the situation as if it were a scenario-type question while incorporating what you know about the real issue. It is therefore a good idea for you to be aware of all the news and challenges faced by your general profession and specialized field, which you would do anyways to prepare for policy or hot topic questions. (See the discussion on these questions for how to stay up-to-date on current issues.)

6. Autonomy support

Autonomy support refers to the right of individuals to make decisions about their own wellbeing. This is referred to as *patient autonomy* in medicine. The health care provider is not allowed to make treatment decisions for the patient as this would violate patient autonomy. Rather, it is the responsibility of physicians to educate and inform the patient using the latest scientific evidence so that the patient can make the most informed decision on their own. An example outside the field of medicine is when lawyers provide expert solutions to their clients. Lawyers can only present possible solutions and outcomes based on their expertise but cannot make a decision on behalf of their client. The same concept is equally important in other professions and in all circumstances in which the professional's job is to educate those under their care based on their expertise in the field so that care receivers can make sound decisions autonomously. People's autonomy to think, decide, and act must be respected. As a professional you must apply this mindset in your daily life and in scenario questions where you are given the role of an expert.

There are only extreme cases when professionals can violate this rule, such as when an individual is not of sound mind or physically incapacitated to an extent that makes them unable to communicate and make decisions. In other extreme cases, such as when someone is likely to cause harm to themselves or others, the ethical obligation to support autonomy is replaced by the ethical and, in some cases, legal obligation to intervene and protect the health and safety of the individuals involved. There are always exceptions to the principles discussed and you must develop the maturity of thought to exercise good judgment and flexibility when faced with extreme cases.

7. Informed consent

Another concept related to autonomy support is informed consent. Once you have provided the best possible solutions to those under your care, you are responsible for answering any and all of their questions regarding the solutions and potential consequences to make sure they fully understand their options and can make an informed decision. Once care receivers are fully informed, they can give informed consent to either receive or refuse a specific course of action. For example, as a nurse, you would have to address all questions about a treatment option, or request the help of a doctor to do so when the questions are outside of your scope of practice, so that the patient is truly able to give informed consent to that treatment. An excellent exercise for you to do right now is to think of at least 5 different professions and come up with examples of how autonomy support and informed consent are integral parts of these professions. Then, apply this to 5 everyday scenarios that involve an expert and a novice or a supervisor and a subordinate.

8. Evidence-based practice

Practicing professionals are expected to make decisions and provide care and expertise based on scientific evidence, rather than gut feeling or personal opinions. In the absence of scientific evidence, the best source of information is experience accumulated in the profession, such as from case studies. Therefore, whether you are a medical doctor, a teacher, a dentist, or a speech therapist, your decisions must be based on sound evidence.

This does not mean that you need to have all the scientific knowledge to do well on a scenario question! Recall that interviewers are not trying to test your background knowledge in a particular profession. Rather, they want to see that you can identify the missing evidence and discuss how different pieces of evidence would influence your next steps. Therefore, you must incorporate evidence-based practice into your fact-gathering procedure in complex scenarios with many unknowns and show that you are capable of making decisions based on evidence. We will discuss how to structure this portion of your answer when we discuss the strategies to approaching all scenario questions later on.

9. Rural vs. city practice

Scenarios set in a rural context require you to address specific concerns. You must have a good understanding of what the challenges are for professionals working in a rural setting and for community members trying to access care, what the advantages and disadvantages are for both parties, whether the care provider or the care receiver comes first when considering these pros and cons, who should decide where someone ought to practice, and so forth. Knowing the answers to these questions will enable you to navigate scenarios that play on this theme with confidence.

10. Legal awareness

This type of question requires you to have common sense awareness of what procedures or actions are legal vs. illegal. In general, the decisions you make must be legally sound in almost all circumstances. We say "almost all" because there may be cases where doing what is legal might cause more harm to those involved. These scenarios are rare, but they are challenging for the unprepared candidate and those lacking maturity of thought because they present a seemingly impossible ethical dilemma. For these situations in particular, it is crucial to identify the most vulnerable party and support the decisions you make by prioritizing their wellbeing and the wellbeing of others who are directly or indirectly involved.

Keep in mind there will also be times when a legal policy brought up in your scenario is outdated and should be systematically reformed. This is why, in countries using the common-law system, the decision-making process in unusual cases can be influenced by a body of unwritten laws based on legal precedents established by the courts. This body of unwritten laws can sometimes become the basis for new legislation to be proposed and enacted. The common-law system is practiced by almost one third of all countries around the world, including the U.S., the U.K., Canada, Australia, and New Zealand. Laws are continuously modified to keep up with the changes in our social environment and advances in technology, science, and general human understanding.

As a disclaimer, note that we are not lawyers and we cannot provide any legal advice because it is outside of our scope of practice. If you want to learn more, you must contact a lawyer. However, remember that your interview is no more a test of your legal knowledge than it is a test of your medical knowledge. Rather, interviewers want to see that you have the maturity to react based on common sense.

11. Alternative solutions

In almost all professions, there are alternatives to generally accepted practices. For example, in medicine, alternative solutions include those provided by homeopathic medicine, naturopathic medicine, and chiropractic medicine. In teaching, alternatives to traditional schooling include homeschooling or boarding schools. You may encounter scenarios that require you to show awareness of alternative solutions and professions and know when and how, if at all, you might recommend such a solution.

12. Non-judgmental approach

Now, this is a special theme because all scenario-based questions fall under this category in some way. As you may recall, we talked about how you need to approach all interview questions using a non-biased approach so that you do not jump to conclusions or take extreme positions. However, some scenario stations will specifically frame an issue in a way that would lead unprepared candidates to make a snap judgment about the situation or the character of an individual involved. For example, you may get a scenario in which a student coming in to seek help from a professor is described as always being late to class and rarely submitting work on-time. Though this might suggest that the student is irresponsible and does poorly in class, you cannot make those assumptions based on the intentionally misleading information. The student could be extremely bright and hard-working but facing personal difficulties that are not revealed in the prompt. Being non-judgmental at all times requires you to be on the lookout for biasing facts in the questions you encounter.

As a quick exercise, think about the last 2 important decisions you had to make quickly about a situation or a person. Did you gather all the facts first or did you jump to a conclusion right away? How was your action influenced by your initial judgment or assumptions?

13. Conflict resolution

This type of scenario, as the name implies, deals with situations that require you to intervene to resolve a conflict. This can be an internal conflict, a conflict between two individuals unknown to you, or a conflict between you and a superior, a colleague, or even someone under your care. The scenarios will vary in detail, but the essence remains the same. You have to show that you are able to maturely and professionally resolve any conflict and come up with an agreeable solution for all parties involved.

14. Global issues related to the profession

There may be scenarios that assess your awareness of global issues that might impact your future profession. Once again, the only way to show such knowledge is to continuously read articles, scientific papers, and reports related to your profession from international governing bodies and other reliable sources. After all, if you are truly interested in your profession, wouldn't it make sense for you to obsess over everything there is to know about it?

15. Cultural sensitivity

As a professional, you are going to encounter people from different cultural, social, racial, and religious backgrounds. Often, such differences lead to different behaviors, expectations, and beliefs and your job is to show your understanding without any judgment while providing the best care or service possible. For example, what would you do if you were a teacher and a student objected to an exam date due to a religious holiday? Would you accommodate the student, or would you remain strict about the exam date? If you do decide to accommodate them, how would you do so while being fair to other students?

16. Empathy

Being sensitive to others' emotions and having the capacity to understand and experience the feelings of others is a critical skill in any profession. When you understand those you serve, you are better able to react and attend to their inquiries, needs, and fears. Importantly, when you are truly empathetic, you can foster a trusting relationship, which in turn promotes better care delivery because those under your care will be more likely to listen to and implement your recommendations.

17. Confidentiality

As a professional you have a moral and even legal obligation to keep all information about those under your care confidential at all time. This means you must not reveal the details of any of your conversations or findings about your care receivers to anyone who is not directly involved in providing care for them, including your own close friends and family members. You have to truly understand and display a genuine appreciation that care receivers are revealing very sensitive and sometimes embarrassing information to you as a professional. Therefore, maintaining confidentiality is critical to maintaining trusting relationships with your future patients. Furthermore, it is important to apply the same principles even in your personal life. If your family members, friends, or peers share confidential information with you, you should appreciate them opening up to you, and importantly, not share that information with others.

18. Beneficence ('do good')

Beneficence requires that you act with the intent of doing good for the care receiver involved. This goes hand-in-hand with the next theme.

19. Nonmaleficence ('do no harm')

Nonmaleficence requires that you act without the intention to harm the care receiver involved or others in society. There are different opinions about the concept of harm or doing bad. In health care professions, a harmful action is one that worsens the condition of the patient. In some cases, it is difficult for health care providers to successfully apply the *do no harm* principle if the action required to achieve it runs counter to their morals and beliefs. Refusing to act in cases like this is called conscientious objection. We will discuss it shortly.

20. Justice

The term *justice* means fairness in treatment. Its opposite, *injustice*, therefore occurs when similar cases do not receive similar treatment. To make just decisions in the context of health care, these four main factors must be evaluated:

   i.   fair distribution of scarce resources,

ii. competing needs,
iii. rights and obligations, and
iv. potential conflicts with established legislation.

21. Patient-centered care

In a nutshell, being a patient-centered health care provider means putting the patients' needs before your own. In the introduction to their article *Ethics, risk, and patient-centered care: How collaboration between clinical ethicists and risk management leads to respectful patient care*, Sine and Sharpe clearly state, "Patient-centered care is driven in part by the ethical principle of autonomy and considers patients' cultural traditions, personal preferences, values, family situations, and lifestyles." The authors continue to explain that when health care providers do not meet patient needs or understand their expectations, the patient may be dissatisfied with their health care services. An additional article by Linda Bell entitled, *Patient-Centered Care* stated, "The goal of patient-centered care is to see the patient and family as a single unit. That is, care for the patient includes the family, and decisions made about patient care include the patient's and family's wishes."

22. Conscientious objection

This is a sincere objection to participate in an act by reason of moral and ethical beliefs that influence one's views on life. Conscientious objection in medicine is highly relevant to cases involving physician-assisted dying and abortion. A health care provider's moral and ethical conflict and disagreement about an act, such as physician-assisted dying or abortion, may prevent them from engaging in such act, although it may be legal in their country, state, or province. In the case where conscientious objection comes into play, it becomes important to respect the physician's autonomy. However, they may still recommend other physicians who would not be in the same conflict, or the patient may need to seek out other physicians who do not have conscientious objections to providing the treatment or procedures they need.

23. Communication

Communication is not only an important skill that you need to demonstrate throughout your interview, it is also a theme in all scenario questions. In any situational question, interviewers are assessing how you gather information from other parties involved in the scenario, how you propose to relay your ideas to them, how you address their needs, how you get them to cooperate with you on your solutions, and so forth. Therefore, you must not only communicate your points clearly, you must also demonstrate that you are able to communicate effectively in hypothetical situations to audiences of different backgrounds.

Most scenario-type questions incorporate multiple themes simultaneously. For example, in a situation involving a patient and physician, themes such as patient-centered care, autonomy support, confidentiality, cultural sensitivity, and so forth can all be at play. The type of situation you encounter will determine how you should navigate it, including what you say to the other parties involved, how you relay that information, and what the best solutions are. Therefore, before you respond to a scenario question, you should always identify the themes as this will help you to formulate an appropriate plan of action. The best way to understand these concepts is to see them in action in sample questions. Therefore, pay attention to the scenario questions in *Chapter XII: 20 Sample Residency Interview Questions with Expert Responses and Analyses* and see if you can identify the themes present in each. You will be able to continue practicing this for the scenario questions in *Chapter XIII: 80 Practice Residency Interview Questions*.

Steps to Answering Any Scenario Question

Given the potentially overwhelming number of theme combinations, scenario- or situation-based questions tend to cause a lot of anxiety for interviewees. However, there is one straightforward structure to use when approaching *any* such question. Knowing it by heart will help you build confidence and competence as you practice. The following steps may sound familiar because they were briefly discussed in *Chapter VI: Pre-Mortem: 18 Proven Strategies to Prepare for and Ace Any Residency Interview*. However, since they are especially important for scenario-based questions, we reiterate them here and encourage you to familiarize yourself with them as quickly as possible.

Step 1: Identify the most pressing issue.

Do not rush a scenario question. Take a step back and identify what the most pressing issue is first to make clear to the interviewer exactly what the focus of your answer is. Whenever you read a scenario, ask yourself "Who are the vulnerable parties?". Their safety and wellbeing should be your top priority and ensuring their wellbeing is the pressing issue you are focusing on. You only have a few minutes to deliver your response, so if you miss this step, you may give a response that is irrelevant or even propose a solution that is dangerous and irresponsible.

If you are having trouble identifying the most pressing issue, think about the consequences of doing absolutely *nothing*. For example, what would happen if someone is inebriated and you let them drive? What would happen if you get into a conflict with someone and you do absolutely nothing to resolve it? What would happen if one of your team members refuses to do their part and you do nothing to address that problem? Often, doing this exercise will help you to identify the individual or group that would be most impacted by your action or inaction.

Step 2: Reserve judgment until you have all the facts.

Next, you have to gather all of the facts prior to formulating a plan of action. Most scenario questions are missing a lot of crucial information. This is done intentionally to see whether you are going to assume certain facts that are not explicitly available. If you are judgmental and make assumptions, your response will lack nuance and you will be viewed as lacking maturity. Mature professionals, like physicians, consider multiple perspectives at once and reserve judgment until they have a complete picture of the situation.

Consider a situation in which you are working in a group setting and one of the group members complains to you that another member is not contributing enough to the project. A lot of information is missing from this prompt. What has each member already contributed? What is considered an adequate contribution? Does each group member have a clear idea of what is expected of them? Is this a one-time occurrence? Is the group member ill or dealing with other extenuating circumstances? Are the two members on good terms with each other, or is there a history of animosity between them? If you jump to a conclusion and say something like, "Well, in this case I have no choice but to report the slacking group member to our professor," then you have already lost all the points for that station because you acted on assumptions without gathering the facts first.

To approach the situation non-judgmentally, you need to explicitly show the interviewers your thought pattern by verbalizing how you would fill in the information gaps. After you have identified the pressing issue for the group work scenario, you might say, "First, without making a hasty decision, I would have a *private*, non-judgmental conversation with the two team members to gather more information. During these conversations, I would ask each group member to articulate their understanding of the work expected of them, and whether they feel adequately supported in completing that work. I would also want to ask each of them for their sense of how the group is getting along, and whether they, or anyone else in the group, are experiencing extenuating circumstances that may impede progress on their part of the work." First, note the emphasis on the word "private". Asking someone sensitive questions in public could embarrass them, so demonstrate your emotional and social intelligence by explicitly saying that the conversation will be private – and make this a habit in your own life as well. The only exception to this rule is when you have to deal with an emergency, and you do not have the time for a private conversation. Next, verbalize the kinds of questions you might ask during your private conversation in the scenario. By posing the right questions in a hypothetical situation, you will demonstrate your information-gathering skills while also highlighting your maturity when navigating complex and sensitive situations.

Step 3: Determine who is directly and indirectly involved.

As part of your fact-gathering and investigation process, you must, of course, identify all the parties that are directly and indirectly involved in the scenario.

For example, imagine a scenario where you are the physician who needs to communicate a piece of information to a patient. Although in the scenario there are only 2 individuals directly involved (you and the patient), the information can, at times, also indirectly affect the patient's family and/or co-workers, your fellow physicians and colleagues, and/or the medical profession at large. For instance, if the news is about the diagnosis of a serious illness, the family and close friends may need to be involved in caring for the patient, and the patient may no longer be able to work, therefore affecting their co-workers. Depending on the illness, the treatment may require a whole team of medical professionals. If, say, it is a unique case, then even researchers from other institutions may get involved.

Mature professionals can identify those who will be directly and indirectly impacted by their decisions. Conversely, those who do not have maturity of thought will only identify those who are directly involved and fail to see the larger ramifications of their decisions and actions.

Step 4: Choose the best solution(s) based on moral, ethical, legal, and scientific reasoning.

Once you have considered a few practical options, choose the most rational solution. This is the one that causes the least harm to those directly and indirectly involved in the scenario, adheres to existing laws and policies, respects professional boundaries, and so forth. You will also need to *explain* the reasoning behind your thoughts and proposed actions. If you have to entertain multiple hypothetical situations and different solutions to each of them, we recommend using the 'if, then' structure. For example, "*If*, I am convinced that my friend is intoxicated, but is only going to their car to grab their phone and call a taxi, *then* I would not interfere and even offer to help them call a ride. On the other hand, *if* I am convinced that they are going to drive away intoxicated, *then...*"

Note that you need to be thinking about all of these elements (what the pressing issue is, what information is missing, who is directly and indirectly involved, and what the best solution is) *while* you read or hear the question from the interviewer. This may seem very difficult, if not impossible, to do within such time constraints, yet these thinking patterns can absolutely be learned, refined, and facilitated over time. This is precisely why perfect practice is so important. As you initially start practicing, follow the step-by-step strategy slowly and methodically in order to solidify the process. Once you are comfortable with it, this process will become faster and more automatic.

Before moving on to the next MMI question type, we would like to share with you **three master strategies from our CEO** that will help you ace scenario-type questions:

1. Start applying these to situations in your daily life. Begin to identify the moral, ethical, legal issues and so forth in the interactions you engage in or observe on your ride home from school, in the grocery store, in the classroom, on the news, on your favorite show, even in the conversation you had with your mother this morning. For the situations you are personally involved in, follow the steps above to resolve them! That is, identify the pressing issue, remain non-judgmental and gather information, and determine all the parties involved *before* acting. For situations you observe, go through the thought exercise of what you would do in the shoes of each person directly involved.

2. Take it a step further and create scenario and follow-up questions from the situations that arise in your daily life as if you were the test administrator! One way to become an expert

in answering scenario questions is to create questions daily. Do this simple exercise for 15 minutes a day for the next 30 days and we guarantee you will notice a significant improvement.

3. Teach these life-changing strategies to your family and friends. You know you have truly mastered a skill when you are able to teach the material to someone else.

These strategies will not only help you ace scenario-type questions, but they will help you become a mature professional and a better person, which is the primary goal of this book.

b. Acting

Another question type that can come up in MMIs is acting or role-playing. At these stations, you are given a prompt that describes a certain situation and your role in it. You are then asked to enter the room and act as if the situation is actually happening, usually by interacting with an actor or another candidate. For example, the prompt could be "Your friend, John, who you've known for 10 years, has invited you to his place to discuss a personal matter with you. Walk in and begin talking to your friend, John." When you enter the room, you would act as if you had just arrived at your friend's house and respond to your acting partner accordingly. Other acting situations you may encounter include delivering bad news to a patient, resolving a conflict or de-escalating a situation, and so forth.

Whatever the situation, you will need to understand your role and your relationship with the others involved and tune into the emotions of those people. Remember to always acknowledge the way the other person is feeling and to take time to listen and empathize with them. After they have had a chance to express their emotions, provide reassurance, and only then begin to offer solutions. Sometimes the actors may be instructed to be highly uncooperative and to continuously attempt to escalate the situation. Your job is to remain composed and to resolve the situation professionally, even if the actor is insufferable, annoying, or impolite. Remember, physicians deal with challenging patients and stressed colleagues regularly and they must always remain calm and collected.

In all acting stations, there are two very important things to remember. First, make sure that the words, tone, and body language you use are appropriate for the situation. For example, if a friend shares a piece of good news, it is completely appropriate to smile and tell her how happy you are for her. In contrast, smiling would be inappropriate during an acting station where your friend told you she just lost a loved one. Secondly, always put yourself in the other person's shoes and verbalize the empathy you have for them. For example, if you have to give someone bad news, it is a good idea to say something like, "I know how difficult this must be for you, and it may seem overwhelming. I will be here to help you through this." Acting does not come naturally to most people, and these stations may feel very uncomfortable at first. To prepare for acting stations, pay attention to the acting next time you watch a particularly emotional scene on television or in a movie, practice delivering both good and bad news in a mirror, ask a friend to roleplay with you, or sign up for one of BeMo's interview preparation programs. With thoughtful preparation, you can enter acting stations calmly and successfully navigate any type of situation.

c. Picture-based

In picture-based stations, you will be presented with a photo or an abstract picture representing a social challenge facing our world today and asked to share your thoughts. For example, you may be shown a picture of a mother caring for her child in a war-stricken country or in a time of famine. Respond to such questions by describing who or what is in the image, for example, people's clothing and facial expressions, the weather, or the dwellings or buildings. Your next step is to succinctly share about how the image makes you feel, and/or explain your understanding of the social situation. When appropriate, you can also demonstrate your empathy and offer solutions. While these types of questions are rare, you should still prepare for them in case they turn up.

You must have some understanding of world issues and hot topics to do well on this type of question. We will discuss how to stay up-to-date on these issues in the section on policy-type questions.

d. Video-based

Video-based questions are also quite rare. In these types of questions, you will watch a short video about a hypothetical situation (much like the scenarios we discussed above) and be asked to explain how you would react. Alternatively, you may see a discussion about a policy and then be asked about your opinion. Whatever the content of the video is, use the strategy for that question type, whether it be scenario or policy.

e. Writing sample

While it is most common be asked to deliver your answers verbally, you may sometimes be asked to write or type your response. Writing stations are used for three primary reasons: 1) to obtain a writing sample from each candidate, 2) to increase the number of independent scores per candidate without increasing the number of interviewers, and 3) to increase the number of candidates interviewed without increasing the number of interviewers. This writing sample gives the decision makers another chance to assess your written communication, a very important skill for a physician. Unlike your personal statement, which you had a long time to prepare and submit, you have a limited amount of time to write your response during an interview, and you certainly will not have a second person to help you revise it. Including an additional writing station also means that each candidate receives one more score and more candidates can be interviewed with no additional cost to the university.

Your approach to these types of stations should be no different from the strategies we have discussed for the various question types. Start by carefully considering the question, your main points, and the organization of your response. Careful planning is important because disorganization in a written essay is much more noticeable than in a verbal response. In addition, remember to leave yourself a bit of time at the end to re-read and edit your response. Be sure to check the essay for completeness and fix any grammar or spelling errors. The program may claim that grammar and spelling will not affect your score, but a polished written response is always preferable to a sloppy one.

4. Policy-Based or Hot Topics Questions

Policy-based or hot topics questions will ask for your thoughts on a newly proposed or controversial policy. Any time you are asked about your views or opinions, there are certain steps you should take to formulate a positive and unbiased answer. Avoid stating your opinion on an issue without first considering all sides of the argument. The best way to approach policy type questions is as follows:

Start with an introduction. This should be a general statement that shows your awareness of the policy, the complexities surrounding the issue, and why such a policy may be proposed in the first place. This shows the interviewer you have a good grasp of the topic being discussed and that you are aware there are multiple sides to the issue. Additionally, referring to any recent news regarding the issue demonstrates your knowledge of current events. To do this effectively, you need to have a good grounding in the current hot topics in the profession of medicine, both locally and globally. You need to set time aside *each week* to browse local and national news websites, as well as your state or provincial medical association websites to ensure that your knowledge is up-to-date. You do not need to be an expert on any of these topics, but you do need to have general awareness and understanding of the key points and arguments.

Once you have introduced your answer and spoken generally about the complexities around the policy at hand, begin examining the specific benefits and drawbacks that need to be considered prior to taking a stance on the issue. At this point, you will outline pros and cons from the point of view of those affected by the policy. Present the positives and negatives from the patient, student, or client's point of view before the positives and negatives for the physician or other professionals. This shows that you consider the wellbeing of those under your care first, before considering what is best for you.

Based on the evidence that you have presented, you will then discuss where you stand on the issue. A common misconception is that the most important part of your response to a policy question is the ultimate decision you make; this is not the case! Instead, what matters most is your ability to articulate your thought process when analyzing a complex issue. When committing to a final stance on a policy issue, it is a good rule of thumb to side with the option that does the most good and the least harm for the most vulnerable parties involved. Alternatively, you can provide a unique solution or compromise that would benefit all parties. Keep in mind that if you take this approach, the interviewer may press you to make a decision. If this happens, be prepared to choose one option over another while providing an explanation for your decision. Again, if you have already discussed the complexities of the policy issue and can articulate why you are making that choice, you will do well on this type of question, regardless of the final decision you make.

In general, when it comes to policy-type questions, avoid starting with your own position on the policy, taking an extreme point of view, providing one-sided answers, or allowing your emotions to guide your response. Take a step back and consider the pros and cons for all individuals affected by the policy. Remember, the way you approach the question and discuss your thought process is far more important than your ultimate decision. These issues are controversial for a reason; there are strong arguments to be made for both sides!

5. Quirky Questions

Sometimes, you get asked a question that just seems, well, weird! Have you ever been asked which organ of the body you would be? Or what superpower you would like to have? How about being asked to teach the interviewer how to do something in a few minutes? These quirky questions are designed to surprise you and throw you off your game. One of the main reasons these types of questions are asked is to see how you react under stress!

Of course, now that you know you can get asked these types of questions, you can develop a strategy and be able to remain calm. Take a step back and plan for a few seconds before beginning your answer. It is always better to gather your thoughts and execute a well-organized response rather than giving an unplanned, rambling answer. Interestingly for these types of questions, interviewers care little about the direct answer to the question. Do the interviewers really want to know which organ you wish to be or what superpower you wish to have? No! What they are truly after is an explanation of *why* you are choosing that particular organ or superpower. You must therefore strategically use your answer as a platform to discuss an aspect of your personality you wish for them to know. Do not just say you want to be a liver because livers are cool. Instead, say you would be the liver because the liver is resilient, like yourself. You can then provide some personal examples as evidence of your resilience, just as we discussed for personal questions above. Do not just say that you wish to go back in time because time-travel is awesome. Rather, say you wish you could go back in time to see your beloved grandmother who passed away a few years ago and learn more from her. As you can see, a strong answer to a quirky question should do more than just answer the question; it should also showcase one or more of your important traits.

What if you are asked to teach the interviewer something in a few minutes? A lot of candidates panic at questions like this because they are unsure what kind of skill to teach in such a short amount of time. Again, it is not *what* you teach but *how* you do so that is important. Choose a hobby of yours, like a sport or fine art, or a language other than English, and teach the interviewer the basics of that skill. If you play tennis, teach the interviewer the proper stance for hitting a forehand, keeping in mind that what you are truly demonstrating here is your communication and collaboration skills. So, break the task down into 3 to 4 easy-to-follow steps and check in with the interviewer throughout the teaching process to see if they have any questions or need clarification.

Take some time to think about how you would answer the example questions above to prepare for these types of quirky questions on interview day.

6. Collaborative or Task-Based Questions

Collaborative questions can take on many forms. You may be asked to work with another candidate or the interviewer to solve a problem, create a plan, teach each other something, argue opposing sides of an issue, act out a scenario, and so forth. In medicine, you will be working with other members of a team, each with their own expertise and responsibilities. You will also work collaboratively with patients to ensure their health and wellbeing. Therefore, you must be able to work effectively with a wide variety of personalities to succeed in this profession.

The key to acing such a question is remembering to *collaborate* with the other applicant or applicants so that you *all* succeed, rather than trying to outshine them. While it may feel as though you are being directly compared with the other interviewee(s), it is common for an entire group to perform very well or very poorly. The best applicants are inclusive, encouraging other interviewees to express their opinions. So, make sure you are not fixated on getting your opinion out there. Listen, engage with others, and solicit feedback!

A subset of collaborative questions are task-based questions. These typically involve a drawing or building task. At this kind of station, you will be asked to describe an image or object to another applicant or the interviewer. The other person will then have to reproduce the image or object without having seen it. Alternatively, you may have to reproduce the image or object another candidate is describing. The drawing or building question is used to assess whether you approach problems in an organized and logical manner, whether you possess strong communication skills, whether you can patiently guide a naive participant through a complex task using accessible language, and so forth. Remember, you will be explaining complex concepts to patients and colleagues in your future career. The interviewer wants to see that you have the ability do so.

The following is an example of images on a sheet of paper you may be asked to describe at a drawing station.

Before you begin, take a step back and orient the other person. Make sure they are prepared with a pen and paper and understand the task at hand. Next, give a general overview of the picture or object they are about to draw. For example, you might say, "Orient the sheet of paper vertically. On it, there is are four equally spaced black-and-white figures arranged in a two-by-two array. The array takes up the top half of the page, and each figure measures about 4 inches by 4 inches." Only after you have properly oriented the other person should you ask them to begin drawing. After each step, make sure to pause and ask the other applicant or interviewer if they are following you or if they have any questions. This is very important. You do not want to spend five minutes describing an image in detail only to find that you lost your drawer after your first instruction! Soliciting feedback from the other person will make you stand out as a candidate who listens and adjusts their strategy to help others achieve a goal.

If you are given a simple line drawing or geometric object, we recommend that you use the Cartesian system of x- and y-coordinates to describe the image to the drawer. To do this, ask them to draw the x- and y-axes along the bottom and left side of the page so that the origin of the graph, (x0, y0), is at the bottom left corner. Then, ask the person to label equally spaced points on both the x- and y-axes from 1 to 9. That way, you know that your scales will be the same, so that the point (x5, y5) will correspond to the exact middle of the page both for you and for the drawer.

Once you have oriented the drawer, you will look at your image and decide how many points it must be divided into. For example, if you had to describe a 1 in by 1 in square at the bottom left corner of the page, you would tell the drawer that the image you would like them to reproduce is made up of four points, which you will call A, B, C, and D. Then, you would say, "Point A on this image is located at (x2, y2), point B is located at (x2, y3)," and so forth. Then, simply instruct the drawer to connect the appropriate dots together to form the exact image. (Note: Choose the most appropriate measurement unit. For example, use inches if you are in interviewing in the U.S., but centimeters in you are interviewing in Canada. Alternatively, you could ask the drawer which system they are most comfortable with.)

Blinded tasks like this one, where one member of a team does not know what the final product should look like, are difficult and designed to test your communication skills and problem-solving skills.

As a future professional, you will often have to make specialist knowledge accessible to non-specialists, so knowing how to break down a complex task or idea is a valuable skill. For a task-based station in your interview, bear in mind that, while the end result is important, the process itself is even more crucial. Using the approach outlined above will make you stand out amongst the other candidates. We recommend that you practice reproducing different types of images with friends and family prior to your interview so that you are fully aware of the potential difficulties that might arise during this process.

On your interview day, another candidate may be given the task of describing an image to you. As you reproduce the drawing or object, be sure to listen carefully to their instructions and politely ask for clarification, if needed. You may find that you have a difficult time reproducing the image because the other candidate is not using a very systematic method to describe it to you. If this happens, you may politely suggest that the other candidate orient you to the bigger picture, or that they use the Cartesian system we have just described. Being able to tactfully assist the other applicant will highlight your leadership and teamwork skills and your capacity to remain calm and composed while engaged in a highly complex task. Displaying these qualities on your interview day will show the admissions committee that you are prepared for a career as a future medical professional.

Although task-based questions are usually collaborative, they can also be used to assess how strong your procedural or dexterity skills are. An example of this is having to reproduce a drawing or diagram while also answering a separate question, for example, "Why are you pursuing this specialty?" This type of question can come up in competitive, procedural-based specialty interviews, for example surgical specialties. To practice this type of question, look at the drawing above. Now practice trying to draw it on a piece of paper while also following the structure for answering "Why this specialty?" This is the type of question that assesses your ability to multi-task and show both verbal and manual dexterity, something surgeons do regularly.

We hope you now have a better understanding of the common question types as well as how to approach them. Remember, the best way to prepare for your interview is to not only learn about the question types theoretically, but to practice using the strategies yourself. You will have ample opportunities to do this in our later chapters that provide sample questions and answers, and practice interview questions. But first, we will supplement this chapter with common topics of debate in medicine to help prepare for policy-based questions, as well as extra preparation tips.

CHAPTER VIII

Common Points of Debate in Medicine and Advanced Preparation Tactics

In this chapter, we give you some extra materials to aid you in your interview preparation. These include a) a list of controversial topics in the field of medicine, and b) ten additional preparation tips from our experts.

Major Points of Debate in Medicine

Familiarizing yourself with the major points of debate in medicine will be valuable to your interview success. You may be asked about these topics directly in policy-based questions or even indirectly in scenario-type questions. Here are a few examples:

- Physician-assisted dying or end-of-life options

- Abortion
- Doctor or pharmacist prescribed birth control
- Vaccinations and whether they should be mandatory
- Legalization of recreational marijuana or other drugs
- Rural vs. urban healthcare
- Compulsory rural medicine service
- Stem cell research
- Genetic screening
- Prescribing medications to friends and family
- Allocation of finite resources (e.g., choosing which patient receives an organ transplant, which patient should receive the first surgery or the only dialysis machine)
- Prescription pain medication, over-prescription and addiction
- Safe injection sites and other harm reduction strategies to combat the opioid epidemic
- Vaping and regulations related to this activity
- Pass-fail vs. using grades to evaluate medical students
- Resident duty hour restrictions
- Fee for service vs. salary and other compensation measures
- Obesity epidemic
- Other current issues in the US, Canada, Australia, New Zealand, Israel, the UK, Europe or wherever you are going to have an interview

The list of topics we presented is not exhaustive of all major points of debate in healthcare. However, we provided you with a number of major topics. By staying up-to-date with these ongoing debates, you will acquire the knowledge necessary to address the issues presented to you in your interview. You can do this by reading the daily news and regularly visiting the websites or social media sites of your local or national professional associations such as the American Medical

Association or Canadian Medical Association. Do not underestimate the time you need to spend reading and learning about such topics. This component of preparing for your interview should begin ASAP because crunching in the information at the last minute is not going to be sufficient.

Bonus Essential Preparation Tips

Here are a few final tips to help you prepare for your interview:

1. In the likely case that your interviewer asks you whether you have any questions for them, you must have a few prepared. This is not only an invaluable opportunity for you to learn more about the program, it is also your chance to demonstrate to the interviewers your commitment and interest in the program. A good question is one that a) you genuinely want to know the answer to, and b) is not obviously answered by the material available on the program website. Formulate your questions based on the thorough research you do on the program in advance. For example, after learning everything you can, you may still have questions about the curriculum, upcoming or recent curricular changes, research opportunities, and so forth.

2. Be prepared to answer follow-up questions about any activity in your application – particularly if it is an open file interview format. You should be able to speak to each component of your application with ease.

3. Listen to yourself speak all the time. Are you overusing words and phrases such as "um", "like", "so", "because", "just", "honestly", "very", "really", "literally", "stuff", "you know", and "thing"? These words need to be eliminated from your vocabulary as they prevent you from coming across as professional, confident, clear, and succinct. We highly recommend that you review *It's the Way You Say It - Second Edition: Becoming Articulate, Well-Spoken, and Clear* by Dr. Carol A. Fleming to learn how to become more articulate, a skill you need for life. We are not personally connected to this book or

its author in any way (i.e., there's no conflict of interest in our plugging this book); we just genuinely find it to be one of the best resources out there for improving verbal articulation!

4. Be cognizant about not speaking ill of others, especially if you are trying to raise yourself up by putting others down. That will have the opposite effect of shedding negative light on yourself! Work on being positive and taking a positive approach to others at all times.

5. In addition to always shedding positive light on yourself and others, always finish each question with something positive, whether that is resolution to a conflict, a way that you grew through a difficult experience, or something that will help you in the future. *Never* end a response on a negative note. Recall how we talked about the primacy and recency effect. You do not want to end your response on a negative note because the last thing you say is what is going to be remembered most by the interviewers.

6. Take full responsibility for all your failures and weaknesses. It is not a bad thing to acknowledge your limitations. What residency programs look for is that you do not make excuses, but take ownership of your shortcomings. As noted above, end on a positive note by saying what you have done to overcome your failures or improve yourself.

7. When preparing for any question or question type, you want to say your answers out loud. Audio tape or video tape yourself, listen to what you said, and revise your response. You will be surprised how different it is to think of a response internally and then hear what you say when you verbalize it.

8. Take your interview seriously and your interviewers will take you seriously. The more preparation you put in using the advice in this book, the better you will perform. Your interviewers will be able to tell that that you prepared, and they will appreciate that you did not take this opportunity for granted. This is a signal to the interviewers that you are ready to take on a professional role, work hard, and learn.

9. Remember you are being evaluated not onl interview but during the whole day. Your staff and current residents are also importa often told to be on the lookout for red flags concerning that candidates say during a ᴜ the interview day. So, remember to stay 'on' the whole day; ask questions, be friendly to other applicants, and remain professional.

10. See the interview as an opportunity, not a barrier. Whereas the rest of your application is evaluated on paper or online, the interview is your chance to share about yourself and show your personality in-person. Take advantage of the interview and enjoy the experience!

We hope that the list of controversial topics and extra tips are helpful to you during your interview preparation. The main focus of the last two chapters has been on the structure and contents of your answers to interview questions. However, there are other non-verbal aspects of your interview that are equally important, but often missed by candidates! We are therefore eager to teach you these skills as well so that you can practice them simultaneously as you prepare for your upcoming interview.

CHAPTER IX

What to Wear, What to Say, and How to Communicate Non-verbally during Your Interview

At your interview, you will be judged on more than your responses to interview questions. Other aspects, such as your appearance and non-verbal behavior, are going to have a sure influence on how the interviewers view you as a candidate. We will go through these one by one to help you prepare for and practice them along with your question responses.

Appearance

Let's begin with your overall appearance. Studies have shown that the impressions formed within the first few seconds of meeting an interviewer can set the tone for the rest of the interview. Within this time frame, one of the most prominent things an interviewer will notice is how you dress. As such, you should make sure your attire and appearance are professional because you want to be remembered for your friendly personality and strong interview responses, not for your fashion choice or lack of hygiene!

Professional attire for a medical school interview typically means wearing a fitted gray, navy blue, or black suit with a white or light-colored shirt or blouse. For some candidates, a necktie might also be appropriate. If you choose to wear a skirt, ensure that the skirt comes down to at least the tops of your knees and no more than 2 to 3 inches above the knee while you are seated. In general, be conservative and choose neutral colors and simple patterns. This outfit should be paired with coordinating dark-colored, closed-toe shoes that are comfortable, as you will likely be walking around a lot on your interview day, and you will not want to worry about pain or blisters. Jewelry should be understated and complement your overall outfit, so keep items other than watches and wedding rings to a minimum. Besides your outfit, you'll also want to be well-groomed on the day of your interview. Keep your hair neat so that it does not obscure your face and wear it in a comfortable way so you avoid absent-mindedly touching it during the interview. Having a fresh haircut is always a good idea but refrain from completely changing your style the day before your interview, as this may cause you to feel self-conscious. Additionally, those with facial hair should make sure that it is neatly groomed. Overall, having the appropriate appearance will not only give you a professional look, but it will also help you make a very good first impression.

Some schools specifically request that their applicants not use any strongly scented products as the scent can be distracting and may cause allergic reactions in some sensitive individuals. Therefore, both male and female candidates should refrain from using perfume or cologne. Also be selective of the body washes and hair products you use as they may be too heavily scented.

Greetings and Goodbyes

As soon as you arrive on the premise, stay in tune with the individuals and happenings around you. You will be greeted by administrative staff, faculty members, residents, and so forth, so don't let your interpersonal skills fall by the wayside. Smile, show excitement about being there, speak politely, and be pleasant with everyone you meet. Also, remember to interact with the other candidates who are there to be interviewed by engaging in light conversation about where they went to school, what they studied, and so forth. If you notice someone is really nervous, teach them some of the techniques you learned from this book. A professional always helps others, even their own competitors.

Once inside the interview room, make eye contact with the interviewer, smile, and offer to shake their hand. Make sure you have a nice firm grip and look the interviewer in the eyes as you say hello and introduce yourself. If the interviewer does not provide their name, it is appropriate for you to politely ask for it to help engage with the person. Of course, if they inform you that their policies do not allow them to share their names, simply accept the terms with a smile and say you understand. However, if they do tell you their name, ensure that you repeat their name. For instance, if your interviewer says, "Hello! I'm Dr. Johnson. It's nice to meet you!" You would reply, "Hello, Dr. Johnson. It's a pleasure to meet you too!" This way you have made a mental note of their name. You can also consciously use their name a few times during the interview. This will come in handy once the interview is over, and you want to leave the best final impression. At this point, it is important that you shake your interviewer's hand again and thank them *by name* by saying something along the lines of, "Dr. Johnson, it was a pleasure speaking with you. Thank you for your time." By simply remembering your interviewers' names and thanking them prior to leaving the room, you will automatically set yourself apart from the candidates who do neither.

Your introduction and goodbye are extremely important to your overall interview performance. Assuming the interviewer pays equal attention to all parts of your interview, the initial and final moments of your interaction will still stand out disproportionately in your interviewer's memory because of well-documented psychological phenomena called the *primacy* and *recency effect*. As you may recall, the primacy effect is the tendency for people to remember earlier events better than latter events, while the recency effect dictates that people remember final events in more detail than events that occurred before. Additionally, there is scientific evidence showing that the magnitude of the primacy and recency effect is modulated by an individual's mood. If your interviewer is in a positive mood, the primacy effect may be magnified. If they are in a negative mood, the primacy effect will be reduced, and the recency effect will be increased in compensation. Regardless, there is no question that either your introduction or goodbye or both will make a lasting impression on the interviewer, so make the most of these two opportunities.

Non-verbal Communication

Of course, the rest of your interview will still matter a great deal. You must continue to demonstrate the strength of your candidacy through both verbal and non-verbal communication. Since we have discussed at length how to deliver strong verbal responses in previous chapters, we will now spend some more time talking about the non-verbal aspect of your interview.

By non-verbal, we mean what you are doing with your body as you speak. Above the shoulder, this includes maintaining eye contact to show engagement, showing appropriate emotions through facial expressions, and nodding to demonstrate your understanding and agreement with the other interlocuter. You should also refrain from laughing or smiling nervously, since this shows lack of confidence. From the shoulder down, pay attention to your sitting posture and also the positioning of your hands and feet. To ensure you have good posture, sit as far back in the chair as possible and straighten your back against the back of the chair. Next, place your feet flat on the ground and place your hands in your lap. Remember not to move around too much in your chair, clench your fists, or tap your toes. While it is okay to gesture here and there to facilitate delivery, refrain from overly grand gestures, touching your face, or playing with your clothes or hair. Just as confident positions alter your brain chemistry to make you feel confident, taking on stressed positions such as having crossed feet or sitting on your hands will also send stress signals to your brain. You can test this by holding one of these stress postures and paying close attention to changes in your physiology. You will likely observe your heart rate going up, body temperature increasing, and your hands beginning to feel clammy.

Non-verbal communication is important not only because the interviewer is paying close attention to it, but because it is largely subconscious and will more accurately reveal your inner mental state. Anytime the verbal and non-verbal messages contradict each other, your interviewer will likely believe the non-verbal message over the verbal one. For instance, if a candidate talks about caring for an individual who has suffered great loss, but their facial expression is blank and their tone of voice is flat, the interviewer will likely regard them as uncaring and uninterested. Overall, your body language accounts for up to 90% of your communication with others. Therefore, you must have excellent non-verbal communication to complement your verbal responses.

To summarize, here are the things you should and should not do in your non-verbal communication in point form. We begin with what you should do.

- Shake hands with your interviewer(s) when you say hello and when you say goodbye. The handshake should be firm but not crushing.

- Maintain eye contact to show confidence and engagement.

- Relax your face and smile. Show appropriate emotions at appropriate moments.

- Nod your head or say "Yes" to show that you are engaging in the conversation.

- Place both feet flat on the floor and relax your shoulders.

- Place your hands relaxed in your lap. Some gesturing may be appropriate if it helps you with your delivery.

- Project warmth, confidence, and interest with your tone of voice.

Here are the things you should refrain from doing:

- Don't stare intently at your interviewer as this will make them uncomfortable

- Don't touch your face or play with your hair as this may be interpreted as a sign of dishonesty.

- Don't slouch in your chair as this posture can make you seem disinterested.

- Don't cross your arms while sitting as it makes you seem defensive and/or disinterested.

- Don't fidget as this is distracting for the interviewer. Wringing your hands or tapping your feet will make you look nervous and uncomfortable.

- Don't laugh or smile nervously when you are unsure about a situation because it draws the interviewer's attention to your lack of confidence.

Your appearance and communication are just as important for interviews conducted or recorded online. Do not make the mistake of slacking on any of the points above just because you are in the comfort of your home or office. You still need to communicate the same amount of commitment and professionalism as you would in an in-person interview! In fact, there are additional factors in an online or virtual interview setting that you must prepare for. These are discussed below.

Internet connection:

You must ensure that you have a strong and stable internet connection for online interviews. If you know that your internet quality is poor, talk to your provider ahead of time about getting an upgrade, opt for using an ethernet cable instead of relying on WIFI, or ask a friend to use their internet for your interview. If you share bandwidth with others, let them know when you will be doing your interview and politely ask them to refrain from engaging in activities that take up a lot of bandwidth (e.g., streaming TV or gaming) during that time. You do not want to be disqualified over a technical difficulty you could have avoided.

Computer set-up:

The interview should be conducted or recorded on a desktop or laptop, not your smartphone. You should consider the positioning and distance of your camera relative to your face and body. To encourage making eye contact and good posture, place your camera at eye-level. That way, you will be less inclined to stare above or below the screen as you speak, and you will be less likely to slouch in your chair. You should sit at a comfortable distance from your computer camera so that your upper torso is visible on screen. You don't want to appear on video as a floating head, and if you are someone who gestures with your hands, you will want your hands to be visible. Use a high-quality microphone and check to make sure it is functioning properly. Lastly, be sure to exit all social media applications and websites on your computer and cellphone so that your interview is not disrupted by sound notifications.

Room set-up:

If your chair is on wheels and rotates, replace it with an immovable chair so that you are not tempted to turn or fidget during your interview, as this would communicate a lack of confidence. The background that is visible on your screen should be fairly clean. We recommend doing the interview in front of a blank, neutral-colored wall, or at least one that is minimally decorated. You do not want something in the background to distract the reviewer from your response, or even worse, influence the reviewer's scoring in a negative way. Also ensure that the lighting in the room is appropriate. You want your face to be well-lit with natural or natural-looking light from the side, rather than from above or behind. This can significantly alter the reviewers' percept of you as a candidate, so it should not be taken lightly.

We highly recommend you test out these settings multiple times prior to your interview. If you know someone who will also be doing their interview in this format, we also encourage you to practice entire mock interviews with them over videoconferencing. Of course, this is exactly how we conduct mock interviews at BeMo, and students who participate in our interview preparation programs do get tailored feedback about this from our experts!

In this chapter, we drew your attention to aspects of your interview that you may have never thought about, including your appearance, introductions and goodbyes, body language, and even the set-up for virtual interviews. While some of these, like what you choose to wear, can be easily managed, others, like your posture and tone of voice, can only be improved with much effort and time. However, all of these aspects will impact your interview score, particularly in categories to do with communication and suitability for the profession. Therefore, you must incorporate these elements into your preparation right from the beginning as you work on the delivery, structure, and contents to interview questions. Once again, we highly recommend that you get expert feedback, especially on your non-verbal communication, because these behaviors tend to be subconscious. An expert will not only be able to objectively point out behaviors that need to be corrected, but also teach you how to work on them.

We have now explored with you how to tackle interview questions of various types in terms of delivery, structure, and content. We have also shown you the details in your non-verbal communication you need to be aware of. If you are feeling overwhelmed by all of this information, or you begin to feel the mounting pressure as you start your interview preparation, we want you to know that a) this is normal given the colossal task you are about to tackle, and b) you can do something about it! In the next chapter, we will give you a number of strategies to help you manage your stress in the long-term and short-term, as well as on your interview day.

CHAPTER X

How to Manage Stress

One of the most common reasons good candidates fail their interviews is that they let their nerves get the best of them. Their sweaty hands are a huge turn-off to the receivers of the handshake, or they have a shaky voice, stumble over words, or cannot form coherent sentences. All of this translates into a perceived lack of confidence and poor communication skills.

Therefore, it is absolutely critical for you to develop strategies to cope with stress. These will help you for your interview and also for the rest of your professional and personal life. In this chapter, we are going to teach you both long-term and short-term strategies for managing your stress. We encourage you to experiment with all of them and choose the ones that work best for you.

Long-term Strategies

Let's begin by discussing some long-term solutions. These are strategies that you can begin to implement in the weeks and months leading up to your interview.

First, it goes without saying that going through the preparation process we have suggested, including familiarizing yourself with interview and question types, practicing in mock interviews, and getting expert feedback, will make you feel more at ease at your actual interview. The more realistic your practice is, the more comfortable you will be.

We also recommend that you visit the school to which you have been invited prior to your interview, and, if possible, ask to be taken around by one of the current residents. You can offer to pay for their time if you have to motivate them to help you explore the campus or department. The tour is extremely helpful for a few reasons. First, you can familiarize yourself with the interview site and surrounding area. That way, you will know exactly where you need to be and how to get there. We even recommend that you take multiple trips to and from the interview site and where you will be staying so you can figure out traffic patterns and any shortcuts. Immersing yourself in the environment and atmosphere will also put you at great ease on your interview day because being there will no longer be a novel experience. If you have time, engage in an enjoyable activity close to the interview site, such as having a nice meal, listening to your favorite music, reading a book, or socializing with a friend. Furthermore, you may learn something new about the program by speaking to a current resident, which may become useful for your interview. Ask them why they selected the program and what they find challenging about it so that if you are asked similar questions during your interview, you will have another perspective to incorporate into your answer. If the interviewer knows you have spoken to current residents to learn more about the program, they will be impressed by the amount of attention you are giving to this important life decision. However, we recommend that you avoid asking a current resident for interview advice directly because a) they may not be at a level to provide mentorship, and b) they actually don't know how well they did during their interview.

Remember, while the interviewers decide if you are a good fit for their program, you are also deciding if the program is right for you. Considering that you are about to invest several years of your life in the program, you need to be happy with all aspects of it, including non-academic factors such as environment and location, access to gymnasium facilities, wellness programs, and so forth. You are choosing them as much as they are choosing you and this mind set will help you to remain confident.

Short-term Strategies

Having done everything you can to manage your stress in the long-term, you may still find that your stress levels rise shortly before your interview. This is normal, so here are some stress management strategies that you can draw upon in the days or hours leading up to your interview. Since different individuals conceptualize stress differently, each person will also find some coping mechanisms more effective than others.

Before we discuss healthy stress management strategies, we want to draw your attention to some unhealthy habits that may develop that will harm you in the long run. These include:

- Smoking

- Alcohol consumption

- Unhealthy eating (e.g., bingeing, not eating enough, overconsumption of caffeine or sugar)

- Self-isolation (i.e., withdrawing from or taking your stress out on friends and family, discontinuing hobbies, and so forth). Of course, if someone is the source of your stress, limiting the time you spend around that person will help.

- Sleeping too much or too little.

- Lack of or excessive exercise. A moderate amount of physical activity, such as weight training, running, swimming, and so forth, has proven psychological benefits like relieving stress. However, exercising to avoid other responsibilities, or over-exercising such that it results in drastic weight loss is not healthy.

Naturally, our recommendation is for you to avoid resorting to the above for stress relief. They are both ineffective and detrimental to your overall health.

Let's now discuss some healthy short-term stress management strategies that you can draw on, starting with what you can do to reduce anxiety and stress the night before your interview.

The night before your interview should *not* be spent reviewing or preparing for your interview. Cramming the night before or on the day of can have detrimental effects on your performance. By then, you should be well-prepared, so relax, enjoy, go to bed early, get a good night's sleep, and wake up early. The minute you wake up on the day of your interview, fill your mind with a positive thought, remind yourself of all the right things you have done in preparation for the interview, and think of the great opportunity that is ahead of you. If it helps, write yourself a motivational note the night before and read it in the morning. One positive thought in the morning can transform your whole day. Of course, take time to have a good breakfast, get ready, and give yourself ample time to travel to your destination. We recommend that you plan to arrive at your interview site at least 30 minutes before your interview is scheduled to begin. You should have mapped out several routes in advance so you know how long the commute will take and what other options you have if the primary route is unavailable due to traffic.

If you feel nervous before your interview, place a clean pen or pencil into your mouth horizontally and gently bite down on it with your back molars. This will force your facial muscles into a smile. Leave the pen or pencil in your mouth for about 2 minutes, take it out for a few minutes, and then repeat for another 2 minutes. Doing this will trick your brain into thinking that you are smiling, and the neurotransmitters that are released in this process will actually put you in a better mood and help you maintain a positive state of mind. The results are more apparent if you do it in front of a mirror. Alternatively, stand in front of the mirror and watch yourself smile. Your brain physiology will change, and you will begin to feel more positive. You can also try leaning back in a chair with your hands behind your head and your feet up, or standing with your arms outstretched, chest out, and head raised. As with the smiling exercise, you can trick your brain into thinking you are relaxed and confident by holding these positions for 30 seconds or more.

Breathing exercises also help to reduce stress. To do it effectively, take a deep breath in through your nose for 5 to 6 seconds, ensuring that you are using your diaphragm so that your belly puffs out, hold that breath for 4 seconds, and then exhale through your mouth for a prolonged 7 to 10 seconds, again using your diaphragm to push the air out. It should sound like an audible sigh as you breathe out. Repeat this a few times. As you may know very well, the prolonged exhalation causes your parasympathetic nervous system to activate and simultaneously tones down your sympathetic nervous system. If you have access to a stethoscope, test this out by monitoring your heart rate as you perform this breathing exercise. As you take a deep breath in through your nose, notice your heart rate increasing. Then, exhale very slowly and notice your heart rate slowing down. Prolonged diaphragmatic exhalation also occurs after a good laugh, cry, yawn, or sigh of relief, which is why you feel more relaxed after engaging in one of these gestures. This evolutionary tool has been harnessed by professionals such as basketball players who take a few deep breaths before shooting a free throw, or soccer players who do breathing exercises before taking a penalty kick. Military snipers are also trained to do breathing exercises before taking a shot because it reduces their heart rate and breathing rate to give them a more accurate shot. You also can take advantage of this evolutionary tool to aid your performance during your interview!

A few minutes before your interview begins, wash your hands with warm water and soap to get rid of any clamminess. It also helps to have a handkerchief in your pocket for wiping your hands before you enter the interview room.

We hope that some, if not all, of these long- and short-term stress management strategies will become useful for your as you gear up for your big day. Thus far, we have focused on what you should be doing before and during your interview. So, in the next chapter, we will complete the discussion by outlining what you should do *after* your interview, because contrary to what most people think, the application process does not end after you say goodbye to your interviewers!

CHAPTER XI

Post-mortem: What to Do After Your Interview

B efore we dive into sample questions, let's complete our review of good interview etiquette by discussing what you should do after your interview. Most applicants miss these important steps because they think they are done once the interview is over, but there are a few things to do yet!

The #1 thing to do after your interview that's missed by 98% of applicants

It goes without saying that you should continue to smile and greet everyone around you as you leave the interview site, regardless of how you think your interview went. There is a good chance that you are still being watched by administrators and current residents, and you want to leave them with a great last impression of you.

The next and most important step is to spend time in self-reflection. Instead of calling your friends and family or celebrating, turn off your phone and find a quiet area to write down everything you remember from the moment you arrived on site to the moment you left the interview. Record all the details about all the interactions you had, the questions you were asked, the answers you provided, the verbal and non-verbal cues you received from interviewers, and everything in between. You have about 30 minutes to do this before the adrenaline and the stress of the situation starts erasing or distorting your short-term memory. This is why detectives get trauma victims to sit down and explain exactly what happened as soon as possible, even if it means asking them to delay grievance. The exercise of self-reflection gives you the chance to record and learn from your mistakes so that you can do even better in the future.

The entire process of interview preparation, from beginning to end, will not only help you with residency interviews, but also with future job interviews. Furthermore, as a future professional, you will be habitually conducting a pre-mortem (what might go wrong) and post-mortem (what went wrong) to continuously refine your skills, no matter the field. As we said at the beginning of this book, our intent is not to teach you a few quick 'tricks' for you to ace your interview. You are honing important skills of critical thinking, communication, self-awareness, patience, perceptiveness, and so forth, skills that make you a better individual overall.

Communication with the Program After Your Interview

Overcommunication with the program after the interview is discouraged. It goes without saying that you should not call or email every day before Match Day to inquire about your ranking. Some programs will even explicitly tell you that they do *not* want ongoing communication or updates from applicants, so make sure you go through all of your existing emails from them to check if this is the case. If not, two forms of communication may be appropriate: thank-you notes and the letter of intent. Let's take a look at these in turn.

1. Thank-you Notes

Consider sending a thank-you email 1
A note like this is especially appropriate it,
had a meaningful conversation with your in.
that this is merely an extension of good wih,
committee's decision.

If you choose to send one, your thank-you ᴄ   be
addressed to the program director who you can senᴄ   .ail to
directly. The email does not have to be long and drawn ᴄ .ᴄ. Simply
express your gratitude for the opportunity to be considered and your
anticipation about your potential future as a resident in the program.
If you had a memorable conversation, briefly describe what it was
about. The following is a template:

> Dear Dr. _____ (name of the program
> director)
>
> Thank you very much for giving me the
> opportunity to interview at _____
> (specialty, program) on _____ (date). I
> particularly enjoyed speaking with Dr. _____
> (name of the interviewer(s)) about _____
> (aspect of the program), as well as meeting the
> current residents. It was a pleasure learning
> about your program and thank you again.
>
> Sincerely,
> _____ (your name)

2. Letter of Intent

The residency letter of intent is a *single* letter sent to the director of
one residency program informing them that their program is your top
choice. Unlike a thank-you email, the letter of intent is a document
that can absolutely have a positive impact on your application (unless
you are applying to Canadian residency programs – see later
discussion).

As you may know, the algorithm used to match applicants to
specific programs takes three factors into consideration:

...mber of available positions for each program

2) The Rank Order List (ROL) of preferred applicants submitted by each program after the interviews have been completed

3) The Rank Order List (ROL) of preferred programs submitted by each applicant after the interviews have been completed

In general, programs want to rank and match with students who also want to rank and match with them, so letting your top choice program know that you would choose them over and above any other program you've applied for may increase your chances of appearing higher on their ROL, maximizing your chances of matching to that program.

Before we discuss how to approach such a letter, it's important to outline the circumstances in which it would *not* be appropriate to send such a letter. These are the following:

1) You are applying to Canadian residency programs. First, these programs create their rank order list on the same day as the interviews immediately after they have been conducted, so sending such a letter even the day after will not change your ranking. Second, these programs require that the match order remain confidential. Therefore, applicants are forbidden to discuss how they have ranked a given school at any point before, during, or after the interview.

2) If you are applying to residency programs in the U.S., you should send a letter of intent to *one* and only one program. Sending another letter of intent to a second or multiple programs claiming they are your top choice would be highly unethical.

3) You do not have a program you strongly prefer over the others. In this case, it would be best *not* to send one because if you end up matching, you are ethically bound to attend that program.

If you do not fall into one of the three categories above, and you feel a letter of intent would help you in your application process, the following are guidelines on how to approach such a letter.

The best time to send the letter of intent is after you have completed all of your interviews and well before the final ranking deadline, which is usually towards the end of February or early March.

As you will be declaring that this school is your #1 choice, your letter must be sincere, you must demonstrate that you have weighed all the options, and the reasoning behind your choice must be laid out clearly and concisely. The entire letter, including the address and your signature, should span at most a page. This is a formal letter, so needless to say, your grammar and spelling must be impeccable, and it must *not* be written in point form. Address and send your letter to the program director, the person who will be making the final decisions regarding applicants. The following is an outline of what you should include in your letter:

Opening:

- Address the addressee by their full name and title.

Paragraph 1:

- Give a self-introduction, including your full name, your status as a current applicant to the program, and the date of your interview.

- Establish that the program is your top choice, clearly stating that you *will* accept the offer to attend if you are matched.

Paragraph 2:

- Provide your genuine reasons for making this program your top choice. You can discuss what aspects of their program, research, core values, or location stand out to you and why these are central to your decision. Outline how this program will help you to achieve your long-term and short-term goals.

- At the same time, demonstrate why you are an ideal candidate by discussing ways you could uniquely contribute to their program and community.

- For both of the points above, be sure to give concrete examples to support your claims about why the program is a great fit for you and vice versa.

Paragraph 3 (optional):

- Provide any favorable updates since submitting your application and interviewing. This might include a new employment or volunteering experience, new publications, upcoming conference presentations, awards, and so forth.

Closing:

- Reiterate that this program is your top choice.

- Sincerely thank them for taking the time to review your letter.

- Sign off formally with "Sincerely,", "All the best,", or something similar and your full name.

You can send the letter as an email or as a PDF attachment to your email. The subject line should be your full name followed by "Letter of Intent".

The bottom line is that programs want to match with students who are motivated, proactive, and enthusiastic about being there. If you are certain that one program is best suited to your needs, interests, and passions, then reach out to them and make your preference known!

Now that we have outlined the dos and don'ts of the residency interview process from preparation to post-interview etiquette, we can finally begin to practice! To ease you into this, *Chapter XII: 20 Sample Residency Interview Questions with Expert Responses* provides you with sample interview questions with sample answers and a discussion of each. *Chapter XIII: 80 Practice Residency Interview Questions* then gives you additional questions to practice everything you have learned so that you can better internalize the strategies and get a feel for timing and flow.

Are you ready? Let's go!

CHAPTER XII

20 Sample Residency Interview Questions with Expert Responses and Analyses

I n this chapter, you will find 20 difficult interview questions, each with an example of a weak response, a strong response, and an expert analysis of these responses.

Throughout the answers, you will see bracketed annotations pointing out the use of different components of the structures and strategies we discussed in *Chapter VII: Proven Strategies to Approach and Ace 6 Common Types of Residency Interview Questions.* You may notice that the strong answers are longer and contain more information than what you might actually include in a real interview response. We did this intentionally to show you a variety of points you *could* discuss in your answer and to help you learn as much as possible during your preparatory process. However, remember that you should be giving concise answers during your actual interview. You will also notice that some answers refer to specific specialties as necessitated by the question. Though these specialties may not be ones that you are interested in, our examples can, of course, still serve as a guide for the actual answers you might give.

After giving examples of a weak and strong answer, we will then discuss the rationale behind the answers, focusing on what was weak or strong about each response.

To get the most out of these practice questions and answers, we recommend you answer each question yourself first, then evaluate your response against our weak and strong answers.

1. Tell me about yourself.

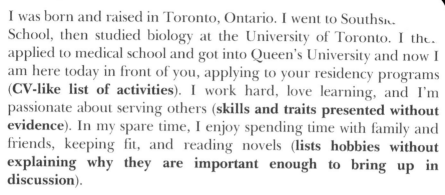

Weak response:

I was born and raised in Toronto, Ontario. I went to Southsiɴ
School, then studied biology at the University of Toronto. I thᴇ.
applied to medical school and got into Queen's University and now I
am here today in front of you, applying to your residency programs
(**CV-like list of activities**). I work hard, love learning, and I'm
passionate about serving others (**skills and traits presented without
evidence**). In my spare time, I enjoy spending time with family and
friends, keeping fit, and reading novels (**lists hobbies without
explaining why they are important enough to bring up in
discussion**).

Strong response:

Thank you for asking me this question. There's a lot I can share about
my life, but I would like to tell you about three experiences that made
a large impact on the person I am today (**sets up structure of the
response**).

First, I was born in Toronto and raised in a tight-knit family. My
parents both work in the health profession; my father is a paramedic
and my mother is a registered nurse. I grew up with them as role
models. They worked nights, weekends, and holidays to serve the
members of our city and community, and they would share their
stories at the dinner table about working with others. They also
shared with me their interest in the medical sciences (**describes first
impactful experience**). From an early age, this built up in me the idea
of pursuing a career where serving others was central (**explains why
it is significant**).

Second, I was always very close to my grandfather. Because my
parents worked long hours, my grandfather often looked after me
when I was young. We shared so many wonderful times together,
taking walks, playing with Lego, and just joking around. When I was
15, my grandfather suffered a stroke. My parents and I rushed to the
hospital. I was so upset and feared for my grandfather's life, but I
immediately felt better at seeing the physicians looking after him.
Specifically, the neurologist in charge of his care took the time to
explain everything to my grandfather and the family, telling us why

vas pursuing a particular treatment. My grandfather was able to e for several years after his stroke, and that time was precious to all of us (**describes second impactful experience**). This made a huge impact on my life in pursuing medicine and, now, neurology (**explains why it is significant**).

Third, when I entered medical school, I pursued research in this field, particularly stroke research. I have been working with Dr. A at Queen's to compile a database of the patients she has treated and the outcomes they have had after various treatments. Not only have I learned a lot about research methods, I have been able to see the impact that research can make on treatments and on patients. Working with Dr. A also sparked my interest in teaching as she was always patient and never hesitated to give me advice and teach me more about neurology (**describes third impactful experience**). I would love to give back in the same way as a teacher and mentor to future learners (**explains why it is significant**).

I have had great role models and mentors in my life and they have shaped me into the person I am: someone who values serving others, critically thinking, and problem-solving, and someone who appreciates teaching (**creative synthesis of skills learned from experiences**). I am here pursuing neurology as I hope to be a competent and compassionate neurologist who puts patients first (**application and future outlook**).

Discussion:

This personal question is commonly asked during residency interviews, so you must prepare for this question well in advance. The goal here is to present your experiences in an interesting and structured way. Taking a look at the *weak* answer, we can see that this candidate merely mentions some of their life experiences and hobbies, without expanding on *why* they chose to bring up these experiences. This example also has no supporting personal details or anecdotes to *show*, not just tell, the interviewers that they are a hard worker, or what they learned from their hobbies. You must resist the temptation to merely recite your CV or list the qualities you possess. Instead, focus on a maximum of three experiences, as in the *strong* answer. This will allow you to use personal examples and details to highlight why each experience was important and to show the interviewer what you learned. The *strong* answer also does a great job of organizing the points in chronological order so that it is easy for the interviewer to follow. Finally, the experiences you discuss do not have to relate to your professional or academic life and can, instead, focus on hobbies or other interests. For instance, you may decide to tell the interviewer about your long-time participation in running. To make the most of this discussion, don't just mention your interest in the activity. Give an example of how you prepared for a particular race or event to show your perseverance, dedication, and any other qualities you feel are exhibited through this activity.

2. Why are you choosing to enter this specialty?

Weak response:

I applied to family medicine because I love taking care of patients on a long-term basis. I also enjoy the broad base of family medicine knowledge and the ability to be a key member of a community who contributes to research, teaching, and advocacy for patients (**lists what they like about the specialty without relating to them personally**). My experiences in family medicine during clerkship solidified this decision for me (**vague statement about experience with no concrete evidence**).

Strong response:

Thank you for asking this question. There are many reasons I am pursuing family medicine, but I would like to focus on three of them today (**sets up 3 points**).

First, I appreciate the continuity of care that family physicians provide for their patients (**identifies first aspect of specialty**). On my family medicine core rotation in an urban setting with Dr. H, I really liked that I could see patients come back and follow up with me. One patient stood out to me. He was newly diagnosed with Type II diabetes and he had many questions about what that meant for his life. Dr. H gave me the opportunity to answer these questions for the patient and explain to him the medication we put him on and lifestyle changes we recommended. I was very glad to be able to see this patient two weeks after our discussion as I was able to answer his questions about the side effects he was experiencing from this medication (**describes personal experience relating to the aspect identified**). I really like that, as a family physician, I will be able to have these long-term relationships with my patients (**reiterates what they like**).

Second, I love that family physicians are educators who teach their patients, colleagues, and mentees every day (**identifies second aspect of specialty**). When I was unclear about how to approach a patient presenting with a headache at the beginning of my rotation with Dr. H, he sat down with me and gave me an outline of how to work through the diagnosis and treatment of various causes of headache. He then charged me with making a presentation on this very topic to the other physicians and nurses at his clinic at the end of the rotation. I was able to solidify my learning by putting this presentation together (**describes personal experience relating to the aspect identified**). This experience showed me how good family physicians are at teaching (**reiterates important trait observed**), and I wish to contribute my knowledge to future learners in a similar way (**shows desire for application**).

Third, family physicians are advocates for their patients, often some of the very best advocates in any community due to their long-term relationships with patients (**identifies third aspect of specialty**). Again, Dr. H was a role model for me here, as I saw him advocate for insurance coverage for medications for his patients almost every day. He would sit down during his lunch hour and respond to queries from insurance companies who seemed hesitant to sometimes cover a particular medication (**describes personal observation relating to the aspect identified**). I know that this type of advocacy made a huge difference for those patients' lives, as they were able to receive the best treatment possible. I was lucky to be able to witness and assist Dr. H with this, and I will certainly strive to do the same as a future family physician (**shows desire for future application**).

I have focused on my core rotation here, but I want to stress that my other family physician preceptors on electives were very similar to Dr. H. All of my experiences in family medicine have solidified my passion for pursuing this specialty and being a contributing member of my community (**mentions multiple experiences confirming their interest**).

Discussion:

This is another commonly asked personal question. Residency interviewers often want to know why you have pursued a particular specialty over all the other options in medicine. Similar to "Tell me about yourself," you should have a well-structured and organized answer with supporting evidence for each reason you mention. Notice that in the *weak* answer, the candidate merely lists things they like about family medicine without any supporting details from their personal experiences within this specialty. You must, instead, follow the example of the *strong* answer, which concisely recounts specific interactions and observations that support each reason for pursuing the specialty chosen. There may be many reasons and experiences that contributed to your desire to pursue a specific specialty. To be concise, choose no more than three experiences or reasons. Go through them chronologically if you can and expand on each reason by providing concrete evidence in the form of a personal anecdote or example. In doing so, you will be showing that you have the experiences and qualities that will make you a good fit for the specialty you are applying to.

3. Why would you like to attend our program?

Weak response:

This is a great program for internal medicine because of the opportunities for research, exploring the different subspecialties, and dedicated time for scholarly activities (**lists advantages of the program without relating to them personally**). I have looked at the matching results your program achieves for subspecialties, and it is very high, so I feel confident I will be able to achieve the career I want after leaving the program (**gives personal motivation that is self-serving**).

Strong response:

Thank you for asking this question. I put a lot of thought into where I would apply as there are many internal medicine programs in the country (**demonstrates that thorough research had been done**). However, in looking into your program, three things really stood out and I feel I would be a good fit for these reasons (**sets up three points**).

First, I really appreciate the extensive research opportunities offered by your program (**identifies first program advantage**). During my years in medical school, I was lucky to be involved in research with Dr. S, a hematologist. I have been working with her to build a database of patients with sickle-cell anemia in our city and keep track of their hospitalizations during pain crises. We are hoping to work with other hematologists and researchers to build a national database, and eventually to improve outcomes for all patients with this condition (**describes related personal experience**). Through your website and in my discussions with current residents here, I was excited to learn that your program also values this line of research. I therefore hope to keep contributing to this research field (**states potential personal contribution**). In general, I deeply appreciate the time residents dedicate to research and the presentation of their work during their rotations.

Second, your program allows residents to get exposure to both general internal medicine rotations as well as all the subspecialties. I also like that there is time to practice both inpatient and outpatient medicine (**identifies second program advantage**). As I mentioned, I have some experience working in hematology, but I would really like to gain exposure to as many subspecialties as I can, as I feel this is the best way to get hands-on experience and know which area of internal medicine I will fit into best. I looked at the curriculum posted on your website and saw ample opportunities to do this (**describes how program would benefit their learning**).

Third, I really appreciate the dedicated time for scholarly activities such as weekly half-days, time to attend lectures and rounds, and study time (**identifies third program advantage**). During my clerkship, I really appreciated those rotations which had this dedicated study time. I found I learned best by combining theoretical and practical knowledge, so I feel your program will be a place where I fit in and learn best (**describes personal reason**). Clinical service and working with patients are the most important roles of a physician, but the only way we keep our knowledge up-to-date is with scholarly activities. Internal medicine is such a vast field, and there is so much for me to learn (**demonstrates understanding of the demands of the specialty and why this structure would be important for succeeding**), so I appreciate that I will have abundant time to do so in your program.

There are so many wonderful things about your program, but the above three are my main reasons to attend your program. I hope to become an internist who serves the community by completing residency here. Thank you for considering me (**summary and demonstration of appreciation**).

Discussion:

This is another personal and program-specific question that is commonly asked. There are many programs, so why would you like to attend *their* program in particular? In the *weak* answer, the candidate simply lists some nice things about the program and ends by focusing only on what they get out of it: matching to their subspecialty of choice. This answer is too shallow, vague, and self-focused. You should, instead, follow the guidelines we used for the previous two questions, which is also evident in the *strong* answer to this question, and pick three reasons for choosing the program that you can expand on. This requires research in advance, so you must take time to read their website and talk to current residents if you can. As you know, you cannot simply state the reasons. Therefore, reflect on the three reasons why that program stands out to you and give supporting details for why each reason makes you a good fit. Try to end your answer by speaking about the ultimate goal you have, which is not just matching to your specialty of choice, but to be a great physician who serves the community. This will draw the focus of your answer away from what you can get out of the program and towards the service you are providing to others. You must have an answer prepared for *each* program you are interviewing at. There can be some overlap in your reasons and examples, as many programs have similar components, but do take the time to read through each program's website and do your research carefully to find out what distinguishes them.

4. Research is an important component of our specialty. Can you tell us about your research experiences?

Weak response:

I agree that research is the way forward for ophthalmology. Without research, we cannot create innovative new treatments and techniques (**demonstrates alignment with value of the specialty**). I have been involved in research with Dr. E at my medical school and have learned a lot about research methods and problem-solving (**no supporting evidence**). I hope to carry this forward during my residency and my career.

Strong response:

Without research, we will not be able to progress in any field of medicine. When I decided to pursue ophthalmology, I knew how important research would be to my future career (**demonstrates understanding of the specialty**). I pursued two separate research projects to ensure I had the foundations to pursue a career in this specialty (**sets up points to follow**).

First, I pursued a basic science research elective with Dr. M whose work focuses on understanding the physiology and anatomy of the eye through studies on animals. My job was mainly to assist with various experimental treatments in the lab. Since I did very little research before this experience, it helped me to get a grounding in research methods, such as setting up a hypothesis, refining the methodology to test the hypothesis, analyzing the results, and even writing grant proposals (**describes relevant experience**). Though I made a lot of mistakes, I was able to learn from them and grow to appreciate scientific integrity through this process (**identifies learning outcome**).

Later during medical school, I pursued clinical research to find the best treatments for patients with glaucoma under the supervision of Dr. L. Shifting to clinical research from basic scientific research gave me the chance to see how our findings were being applied to improve health outcomes for patients. Working for Dr. L involved a lot of face-to-face time with patients, and she taught me how to improve my communication skills so the results we were tabulating were reliable.

I was able to present a poster on our research at my medical school's student poster fair (**describes another relevant experience, respecting chronological order**). Combining my experiences in these two areas of research showed me how innovation in one area leads to progress in another, and that research is vital to bettering health care for our patients (**outlines overall learning outcome**).

I love that your program has dedicated time for senior residents to pursue research (**relates points discussed back to the program**), and I hope to continue contributing to medical research by finding my own area of interest during residency and completing a project that leads to a publication or presentation, and most importantly, improves patients' lives (**outlines personal contribution to this area**).

Discussion:

This is a program-specific question that is personal. You may expect programs to ask about particular experiences or qualities they wish to see in their specialists, especially if, for example, you are applying to a research-heavy program like internal medicine, a specialty that focuses on procedural skills like a surgical specialty or anesthesiology, or a specialty that values communication skills, such as pediatrics or psychiatry. Begin reflecting now on the nature of the specialty you have applied to and what skills and experiences you have that demonstrate your fit for it. In the *weak* answer, the candidate merely states that they have some research experience without supporting evidence. In the *strong* answer, the candidate has followed the approach to personal questions by providing evidence of the type of research they participated in and what they learned from these experiences. The candidate also focuses on the most important part of research, which is improving patients' health outcomes. Finally, the candidate ties their experiences back to the question by mentioning how the program values research and how the curriculum will help them carry forward with research activities in the future.

5. How do you deal with stress?

Weak response:

I do often find myself getting stressed out and sometimes getting upset with my loved ones (**potential red flag**). I understand stress is a part of life as a physician and I try to work out or something to relieve stress (**acknowledges relevance of the question to future career but is vague about their approach**). I'm not sure I yet have a handle on this, to be honest (**does not demonstrate ability to effectively handle stress**)!

Strong response:

Stress is a part of life and certainly a part of our profession. Physicians can work long hours and have many commitments. Emergency medicine especially can be quite stressful as you are constantly seeing patients with potentially life-threatening complications (**acknowledges relevance of the question to future career in the specific specialty**). Over the years, I have developed some coping strategies that are helpful to me during stressful times (**demonstrates confidence in ability to cope with stress**).

One time I felt particularly stressed was during my surgery rotation. This was the first time I was on call during clerkship. I was not getting enough sleep, and I had to learn so much as we switched from one specialty to another during the rotation. We also had to keep studying for our final rotation exam. I felt my anxiety rising and found myself having a harder time falling asleep (**describes relevant experience**). At the mid-point of the rotation, my preceptor had a sit-down with me to discuss my progress. Although I felt a bit nervous about sharing my feelings, I told her about how the stress was affecting me. She was so understanding and gave me some great tips. One of the most helpful things she shared with me that I do to this day is making a schedule a month in advance with all my call schedules, study times, and even time for working out and meal preparation. She also encouraged me to take mini breaks, even if it's just 5 minutes, to meditate during busy call shifts (**describes positive learning outcomes**). I was able to use these skills during other rotations during clerkship, and felt I handled them much better and did not get so anxious or sleep-deprived (**demonstrates ability to apply learning to similar situations**).

I am going to keep using these strategies as I move forward during residency. I feel comfortable monitoring myself for symptoms of stress and reaching out for help if I need it (**future application**).

Discussion:

This is a personal question that asks about your ability to handle a very common part of residency – stress! You can expect to be asked questions about the various challenges you may face during residency, such as lack of time, working on multiple priorities at once, and so forth. In the *weak* answer, the candidate did not discuss any tangible strategies and even mentioned getting upset with others, a red flag. Instead, anytime someone asks you about challenges or limitations, you want to discuss an example where you took a proactive approach. Take a look at the *strong* answer, for example. The candidate knows stress is a part of the specialty they have applied to and speaks about it candidly, giving a specific example of a time they felt stressed and, most importantly, how they overcame it. The candidate also anticipates being stressed in the future and has strategies in place to cope with similar situations, should they arise. The individual who gave the strong answer is clearly someone who is well aware of the challenges within the medical profession and is ready to face anything head-on.

6. What is one challenge you see facing our specialty within the next 5 years?

Weak response:

I feel that one challenge is that patients don't have insurance and they don't have enough money to cover medical expenses, so they end up in debt (**identifies a challenge**). I think physicians in family medicine must be aware of this and distinguish who has insurance or not (**a non-solution to the problem**). Also, people with insurance can get in-hospital care, while those without may not be able to, except for in emergencies (**points out a consequence of the issue without proposing any solutions**). This is just one challenge facing family medicine but there are many others.

Strong response:

This is an interesting question. While gaining experience in family medicine, I have seen many challenges faced by patients and physicians (**relates question to personal experience**). One of these is the divide between urban and rural areas, and the resources available in each (**identifies a challenge**). I grew up in a rural area myself, and I saw the lack of health care resources in my community. For example, my grandfather was diagnosed with pancreatic cancer during my undergraduate years, and he needed a highly specialized Whipple surgery to remove the tumor. The closest surgeon was 300 miles away, and my grandfather waited months to get an appointment with this specialist. The cancer was, of course, growing during this time, and by the time my grandfather made it to the appointment, his tumor was too large to operate on. He passed away one month later. We don't know how long he may have lived with a timely operation, but surely this would have given him a greater chance at survival (**describes a personal experience with the challenge**). I personally have participated in advocacy for increased medical resources and access to care in rural areas during my time in medical school. I pursued rural family medicine electives and during these rotations, I spoke to local politicians about combating this issue (**outlines steps already taken to tackle the issue**). I hope to continue my advocacy for patients in rural areas as I move through residency and into my career (**demonstrates willingness to continue to be a part of the solution**).

Discussion:

This is a policy-type question that asks you to identify challenges facing the specialty you are applying to. This answer requires appropriate knowledge and reflection on specific challenges facing your specialty. First, pay attention to the question. If, like for this question, you are asked to discuss an exact number of points, you should do just that, no more and no less. Next, identify a challenge that you yourself have observed or experienced. If you look at the *weak* answer, you can see the candidate picks a challenge that is potentially controversial, and they also do not provide any examples or proactive plans to tackle it. The *strong* answer provides an example of a challenge the candidate has personally experienced. They also discuss what they have already done to address the issue and what they will continue to do to tackle it in the future. Always outline what you yourself could do to tackle any challenge you name as this shows you taking responsibility and not assuming it's someone else's problem. Please remember what we advised in the discussion of policy questions earlier in the book: You must stay up-to-date with current events and hot topics in the specialty you have applied to so you are prepared to answer any policy-type question.

7. What is your approach to conflict resolution?

Weak response:

I try to avoid conflicts, but what I often do when people disagree is tell the other person what I think first (**red flag: not considering perspective of others**). I try to get my opinion out there before the other person can give theirs, as I often find that conflict leads to heated emotions and then people stop listening. If the other person remains calm, I would carry out a discussion with them. Otherwise, I walk away and hope to resolve the conflict later (**another red flag: judgmental and dismissive approach**).

Strong response:

Medicine is stressful and conflicts happen, whether with colleagues or patients. General surgery is definitely stressful at times, and surgeons work collaboratively with others all the time, whether in the OR or in the clinic (**acknowledges relevance of the question to the specialty**). To resolve conflicts, I rely on the lessons I learned from experiences in the past.

For example, I was the assistant on a research project responsible for analyzing lab results in kidney cancer patients. When I shared my preliminary results with my supervisor, Dr. B, I felt I had done a thorough job with my work and my explanation. However, Dr. B said my results made no sense and he did not think my project was going anywhere (**describes a relevant past experience involving conflict with a superior**). Although I felt a bit upset, I value Dr. B's opinion a lot because he is a very experienced researcher and clinician (**shows respect for the other party, non-judgmental attitude**). So, I went back to my presentation and updated my PowerPoint with a clearer outline of what I hoped to achieve and clarifications of areas that were confusing (**demonstrates ability to self-reflect**). I then met with Dr. B to discuss his feedback with him in person. During this conversation, he gave me various suggestions for different ways I could present my data, but he also said he was going through a tough time the day of my presentation. He apologized for his comments, and we went through my presentation and collaborated to improve it (**describes how conflict was successfully resolved**).

I learned that you must not get upset or judgmental if someone disagrees or questions you. Instead, you must reflect on any errors or mistakes you could have made and openly seek clarification from the other person. Then, you can to work through the conflict together (**outlines lessons learned**). I hope to keep using this strategy moving forward whenever I encounter conflicts during my general surgery residency (**future application**).

Discussion:

This is a personal question that asks how you would deal with a common situation that will certainly occur during your residency training. Note that in the *weak* answer, the candidate not only gives no supporting examples, but actually makes some red flag statements that show a disregard for other people's opinion or point of view. Even though the question does not ask for examples explicitly, you should still supply them, following the structure for personal questions, as the *strong* response does. That candidate acknowledges that the type of situation brought up by the question actually does occur in the profession, therefore validating the question itself. They then succinctly describe an example where they faced such a situation and tells the interviewer what they did to overcome it. The candidate concludes their answer by focusing on learning outcomes and the future application of the approach they highlighted. Throughout their answer, they have shown not only their ability to handle conflicts maturely, but also their ability to learn and grow from their experiences. Take the time now to go through your experiences and pick out specific examples of times you showed important qualities and skills that a resident in your specialty must display. On your interview day, you should have a bank of examples that you can readily use at any time.

8. Consider the following scenario: You are a second-year resident, and your preceptor, Dr. Smith, is constantly berating you, other residents and staff, and even patients. One day, he even calls you an "idiot" and storms away from you. What would you do in this situation?

Weak response:

In this situation, I would approach Dr. Smith and tell him he is being very disrespectful of everyone around him. I would tell him his actions are inappropriate (**confrontational approach**). I am only a resident here, however, so I don't think I would take any further action right now (**doesn't take responsibility**). Perhaps if he does this again, I would report him to my residency program director (**drastic action without first assessing situation**).

Strong response:

Here, I am a resident working on a rotation with Dr. Smith, who is displaying what appears to be unprofessional behavior (**recap of the scenario**). In this specific scenario, my primary concerns are the patients' and my colleagues' safety and wellbeing. I am also concerned about the wellbeing of Dr. Smith, as he may be going through a difficult time which is causing him to make these comments. I would also wonder if I could continue to learn in this type of environment (**identifies pressing issues from multiple perspectives**). The first step I would take is gathering information in a non-judgmental manner. I would first speak to colleagues to see if this has been a more recent issue or if it had been on-going for a while. I would also ask the patients if any of them noticed these comments, and if they were affected by them. I would, of course, try to have a private conversation with Dr. Smith and calmly ask him to please explain the comments I heard (**gathers information**). Once I have gathered information, I would be able to consider some paths forward. It's possible that Dr. Smith was having a very stressful time lately for reasons unrelated to work (**first hypothetical situation**). If this is the case, I would empathize with him, see if I can offer help in tackling stressful situations, offer him resources to help deal with the stress, all the while emphasizing the importance of professional behavior (**first solution**). If this behavior had persisted for a while, I would again see if Dr. Smith was experiencing some kind of stressor and offer him the same help and council (**second hypothetical situation and solution**). If his behavior did not change following our discussions, I would certainly consider reporting Dr. Smith to an authority figure like another attending physician, my residency program director, or a hospital administrator (**third hypothetical situation and solution**), especially if it was negatively impacting our patients. I would not wish for Dr. Smith to be in trouble, but my concerns here are for the safety and wellbeing of patients and staff, and for Dr. Smith to receive the resources he needs to continue practicing professionally (**reiterates pressing concern**). As I move forward in my rotation, I would keep an eye out for any other instances of unprofessional behavior (**outlines further preventative measures**). In summary, I would keep the patients' and my colleagues' wellbeing at the forefront of my mind and work to gather information without jumping to conclusions prior to coming up with solutions to this situation (**summary of approach**).

Discussion:

This is a scenario-type question. The candidate who gives the *weak* answer takes a judgmental approach by assuming Dr. Smith is intentionally being disrespectful and stops short of taking any real steps forward in solving the problem. The *strong* answer follows the guidelines we suggested for answering scenario questions earlier in this book. You will note that the candidate identifies their primary concerns and focuses first on the needs of others. They take a step back and gather information non-judgmentally, then lay out at least two possible paths forward based on the information that was gathered. The solutions offered are communicated with empathy and are designed to address the primary concerns which were identified at the beginning of the answer. The candidate even includes a follow-up step ensuring vigilance on their part moving forward. Finally, they include a concise summary to recap their approach. This is a complete, well-organized answer to a scenario question, and you should aim to practice answering scenarios in this way.

9. If you had infinite time and money, what would you do?

Weak response:

This is an interesting question. I think I would just travel (**identifies activity**). I love traveling and have visited 20 countries in my life. If I did not have any money concerns, I would spend my time experiencing new places and cultures with my loved ones (**gives only selfish motivations for wanting to pursue activity**).

Strong response:

This is a very interesting question. After reflection, I believe I would choose to do two particular activities. These activities reflect my primary goal in life, which is serving my community (**choice driven by life values that align well with the medical profession**).

First, I would still want to pursue residency in this specialty, as I think I am fortunate to be in a profession I love and I have the ability to serve others (**identifies first activity, demonstrates commitment to the field of medicine**). I would still pursue pediatrics, but I think I could then shape my career to work specifically with those who are underserved and lack insurance. Since I don't have to worry about earning money and have lots of time, I can use my time and energy to ensure they get the care they need (**demonstrates selflessness**).

I would also hope to serve more globally. There are so many underserved countries and populations all over the world, and my expertise as a pediatrician and my resources will help me to improve patient outcomes in other locations (**continues to demonstrate selflessness and desire to serve others**). I do love traveling and forging connections with people from different cultures, so serving around the world would help me do more of that (**identifies personal reason for pursuit of second activity**)!

Discussion:

This is a quirky question. A quirky question is a great opportunity to showcase some of your personality and values. In the *weak* answer, the candidate just says they would travel, but this is a very self-centered response. At no point do they talk about why they enjoy traveling or how they can serve others while traveling. In the *strong* answer, the candidate focuses not on what they would do but on the underlying values guiding all the decisions they make. The most important thing to them is serving others, and this leads them to pick the two activities that would allow them to do that if they had infinite time and money. Notice that the candidate still talks about their love of traveling but explains why they enjoy it and focuses on how they will use this opportunity to help others, not just themselves. Take some time right now to reflect on what your values are and what you would do with infinite time and money.

10. Teach me something in the next 2 minutes.

Weak response:

I don't really have anything I can teach, sorry. I don't have any interesting skills (**panic reaction**). Um, I guess I can teach you how to hit a forehand, since I play tennis. OK, so you would hold your hand out to the side like this and swing this way (the candidate would swing their arm). Can you repeat that? (**no clarification, no stepwise approach, does not solicit feedback**).

Strong response:

I would like to teach you to how to say a few words in Hindi, if that is alright with you (**identifies the task clearly**). If I am not clear about anything, please let me know (**asks for feedback proactively**). I am going to teach you how to count to three and we will be repeating each word before stringing them together. The Hindi word for *one* is "ek". Can you repeat it for me? Great! The word for *two* is "do". Can I hear you try it? The word for *three* is "teen". Same thing, I would love to hear you say it back to me. Thank you. Now, let's put it together: "ek, do, teen" (**step-by-step instructions**). Great, it sounds like you have it! And that's how you say *one, two, three* in Hindi. Do you have any questions or feedback for me (**asks for feedback at the end**)?

Discussion:

This is a tricky question, one that our students struggle with occasionally during our preparation programs. Candidates often think they have nothing to teach the interviewers, get flustered, and fumble at the beginning of their answer before giving rushed, unclear instructions on how to do a task, as exemplified in the *weak* response. Remember, what you teach does not have to be a complicated skill, just something simple but unique. Think hard about your background, extracurricular activities, and interests. Do you play a sport, speak another language, play an instrument, or have a hobby? What is a basic part of that activity that you could easily teach someone of any age in three steps? Once you have settled on what you will teach, you must think of this as a collaborative task. As the candidate does in the *strong* response, prepare the interviewer by telling them what you are about to teach them. Then, guide them by giving clear, step-by-step instructions and checking in regularly to ensure they are keeping up with you. This way, you are teaching them something *and* using your communication skills to keep them engaged.

11. Tell me about a time you did something you regretted.

Weak response:

I don't usually regret the things I do because I try to make sure I do them right the first time (**avoids answering the question at first**). If I had to pick one, it would be the time I missed a deadline to hand in a major assignment in my first year of medical school (**identifies an example**). I was still adjusting to my new environment and workload, and I simply forgot to set a reminder for myself. I remembered a few hours later so I submitted it then and went to talk to my professor about it the next day. Thankfully, he was very understanding, so it didn't impact my grades at all (**describes how situation was overcome, no lessons learned or how the same situation would be handled in the future**).

Strong response:

In my first year in medical school, my grandmother fractured her hip and had to undergo surgery. At the time, I was having trouble adjusting to my new environment and workload, so I decided to prioritize my studies over going home to see her. Though her surgery was successful, she died of a stroke soon after and I never got the chance to say goodbye (**clearly identifies a personal example**). This experience really made me rethink my life priorities. Though for a student, academics is extremely important, I came to value my family and friends as well their health and wellbeing much more (**lesson learned**). If I were to encounter something similar again, I would handle the situation very differently. I would definitely do my best to be there for my loved ones in their greatest time of need, even if I had to set aside my work temporarily. However, I would try to minimize the impact this might have on my studies overall by being upfront with my professors about the issues I was facing and asking for extensions on deadlines so I could take care of my family. I would also reach out to my peers for help with taking down notes and catching up with the materials afterwards (**applies lesson by outlining tangible steps to avoid same mistakes in the future**). I think having the ability to prioritize the right things while still taking full responsibility for everything I do, and the outcomes of my actions makes me well-suited to handle the multiple demands placed on healthcare professionals (**application of approach to medicine**).

Discussion:

This is a personal question that asks about a negatively charged experience. The candidate who gave the *weak* answer appears defensive at first, and their entire response takes a dismissive tone. Though the candidate eventually gives an example, they were unsuccessful at highlighting what they did proactively to move past it. They also failed to discuss the overall lessons they learned from the experience and how these lessons might be applied in their future. It's normal to feel uncomfortable discussing negative experiences and emotions, but it's important in this case to show humility and vulnerability. The candidate who gave the *strong* answer was able to do this by not hesitating to open up about a true regret. More importantly, they discussed what they learned from the experience, how they would handle it differently, and why their approach to such situations will be important for a medical professional.

12. Our top priority is the generate awareness and care for those in underserved communities. How will you contribute to this?

Weak response:

I've always been very passionate about underserved communities (**no example to demonstrate passion**). I think it's important for those in the medical profession to help them in any way possible (**vague, cliché statement**). For example, there could be programs set up to make sure they have access to medical resources and mental health resources. Residents can also volunteer their time to understand the needs of different groups in the area and present their findings in educational seminars (**outlines two general solutions, no personal involvement**). Overall, I think there's a lot we could do if we just put in the time and effort.

Strong response:

I have followed the many initiatives of your school to advocate for the underserved communities in this area (**demonstrates understanding of the school/program**). One of the programs I'm particularly interested in is your collaboration with the local women's shelters to provide free health care and counselling to low-income single mothers and victims of domestic abuse (**identifies specific initiative**). I have been volunteering at my city's women's center for a number of years now. During this time, I met countless intelligent and strong women who were struggling against the glass ceiling our biased society has placed on them (**connects to personal experience**). I've come to gain a better understanding of the kinds of prejudices and misconceptions held against these women that rob them of opportunities for employment and welfare that are available to the rest of us. I hope to use my knowledge in medicine to provide basic care to this underserved population at the women's shelters in your area, and I will use my privileged position to continue to advocate for their rights (**candidate outlines how they will personally contribute**).

Discussion:

For a question that asks you how you would contribute to a program or the community, it is crucial that the contributions you discuss are both personal and tangible. The *weak* response does neither. The candidate begins by stating they are passionate about the population brought up in the question, but does not give an example to *show* that this is true based on their past actions. When discussing ways to contribute, the candidate also does not take ownership of the ideas they are proposing, relegating the tasks to the general body of residents or potentially the program to complete. In contrast, candidate who gives the *strong* answer leads with a demonstration of their understanding of the school's values and commitment to this population. They are able to relate a specific initiative of the school to one of their personal experiences, and then outline two ways they can contribute to the cause.

13. Consider the following scenario: You are the coach of a competitive cheerleading team. Your 17-year-old niece is an emerging talent on your team, but her mother, your sister, does not want her to continue pursuing this extreme sport due to the high risk of injury. What would you do?

Weak response:

I would definitely prioritize my niece's health over the success of my team because we're family (**identifies the pressing issue but cites personal motivation**). I would respect my sisters' wishes because she knows what's best for her daughter, and I wouldn't want to jeopardize our relationship (**does not consider the person most directly involved, no gathering information**). However, I would probably let her tell my niece because I wouldn't want my niece to think it was my idea (**not taking responsibility**). If my niece gets upset about her mom pulling her off the team, I would try to calm her down and explain to her that she wouldn't be able to focus on the routines anyways if she didn't have her parents' support (**fails to acknowledge the individual's feelings and opinion**). I think this is the best way to maintain a good relationship with both individuals (**self-focused motivation, once again**).

Strong response:

As a coach, my concern is, first and foremost, for the health and wellbeing of my cheerleaders, and only after that am I concerned about the success of my team (**identifies and two pressing issues and prioritizes them**). Therefore, I would always ensure that all the safety measures are in place during practice and competitions, and that my cheerleaders are not taking any unnecessary risks, regardless of whether their parents are concerned for their safety (**shows how they would ensure top priority before other considerations**).

Since it is an extreme sport, though, I can completely understand parents' concern (**acknowledges others' perspective**). However, rather than making a decision based on my judgment or that of the parent, in this case my sister, I would first want to have a candid discussion about this with my niece. As a mature 17-year-old, she should have the ability to make the decision of whether to pursue cheerleading on her own, and as her coach, mentor, and family member, I would respect that decision (**acknowledges autonomy of the person to make decisions**). I would first want to have a private conversation with her to let her know about her mother's concerns, reiterating the potential risks of the sport, which she should be well-aware of already. I would then ask her what she thought about this and whether she wants to continue with the activity (**seeks information from party directly involved**). If she decides that she would rather stop cheerleading for health or other reasons, then I would, of course, respect her decision (**first if/then**). If she has weighed the pros and cons and is still determined to continue participating in the sport and on my team, then I would sit down with both her and her mother to discuss the matter openly with both of them. I would give my sister a chance to explain why she didn't want my niece to continue the sport. I would let my niece explain her reasoning for wanting to practice the sport to her mother. I would also reassure my sister about all the safety measures we have in place, while also encouraging her to respect her daughter's autonomy in making this decision (**second if/then**). Overall, my approach to this situation is to always prioritize my team's wellbeing, make sure I understand everyone's stance about the issue, and ultimately, to respect and support my niece's choice since she is the one most directly impacted by the decision (**summary of approach**).

Discussion:

Just like for medical scenarios, the same structure can and should be applied to a non-medical scenario. You must identify the pressing issue, remain non-judgmental and gather information, and outline two or three hypothetical situations and your solutions to each of them. In the *weak* response, the candidate seems to be driven by a self-serving need to maintain good relations with all parties, rather than have a genuine concern for the wellbeing of others. They dismiss the opinions of the individual who is most directly involved and impacted by this situation, the niece, and even appears hesitant to take on responsibility. Needless to say, they did not consider multiple hypothetical situations, and it is unclear whether the single solution they proposed would have been effective at resolving the issue at hand. On the other hand, the *strong* response demonstrates the candidate's maturity in balancing conflicting interests. They are able to clearly identify their role and their responsibility for the wellbeing of those under their care. They are also able to consider the perspectives of each and every person directly involved. The candidate also simultaneously takes an active role in the solution while respecting the opinions of the other parties. For all scenarios, you will also want to demonstrate your maturity by considering multiple perspectives, managing conflicting demands, and being empathetic to each party involved.

14. What are your thoughts on how your federal government handled the novel coronavirus outbreak?

Weak response:

I think my government has handled the outbreak very poorly compared to some other countries (**judgmental approach**). They really shouldn't have downplayed the situation earlier on because it misled the public into thinking that the outbreak wasn't a big deal or that it wasn't real. I also don't know why they didn't prioritize testing before it got out of hand, as that would have helped us to get a more accurate picture of the spread and get it under control (**highlighting only CONs**). Things would have been much better if they hadn't ignored the advice of scientists and doctors (**solution cast in negative tone**).

Strong response:

Since the outbreak began to spread globally in January, governments have responded differently in order to slow and contain the spread of the virus in their respective countries (**introduction showing broad awareness of the issue**). Notably, the Trump administration's approach was to downplay the severity of the situation early on, and only later to increase testing power and the supply of medical equipment. Furthermore, the administration has allowed state governments to independently determine measures on social distancing and economic closures (**clear outline of what the government's approach has been**). On one hand, deemphasizing the disease at the early stage may have prevented unnecessary panic and hoarding of important medical supplies, and delaying investment into testing and supplies could have saved the government money in the case that the disease could be brought under control. Also, giving states the autonomy to make decisions about social distancing and closures does afford them with the flexibility of creating policies that cater to the local situation and local needs (**PROs**). However, the administration's reactive, rather than proactive, approach in dealing with this highly infectious disease has now resulted in a severe shortage of testing supplies and personal protective equipment for medical staff on the front lines and the loss of tens of thousands of lives. Some states are also reopening businesses prematurely, going against the recommendations of health officials and putting more lives at risk (**CONs**). I therefore believe that the U.S. federal government has handled this outbreak poorly in comparison to some other state governments (**takes a stance**). A better way to contain such an outbreak like this would be to transparently and accurately relay information about the disease to the public to prepare them for the outbreak and simultaneously equip medical professionals with the tests and protective gear they need to combat the disease. I also think that having government mandates at the federal level regarding social distancing and economic closures would be more effective since it would ensure that all states are following the same guidelines (**outlines alternative approach**).

Discussion:

From time to time, you will encounter questions asking you about policies and issues that you think are "obviously" good or bad, or that you have a strong personal opinion about. It is especially important in such cases that you *not* take a stance right off the bat and come off as judgmental. This is exactly the mistake made in the *weak* response. The candidate begins their answer by stating a strong negative opinion about the issue at hand. They then continue to highlight only the downside of the policies and actions without acknowledging the potential reasons why those actions were taken. The "solution" is phrased in a way that focuses on what should have been done in the past, which is not constructive to improving the circumstances at hand. The approach taken by the candidate who gives the *strong* response is markedly different. While it's clear that this candidate has an opinion, they reserve that opinion until *after* they have discussed general points about the issue and outlined both pros and cons. In this way, they are able to demonstrate that they can evaluate both sides of an issue without obvious bias, giving credit to an "obviously" poor response to the pandemic. This candidate also frames the solution as something that can be applied more broadly to disease outbreaks in general. Though the stance these two candidates take are exactly the same, their approach to the response sets the latter candidate apart as being much more mature and professional.

15. What is one cultural barrier you've had to overcome?

Weak response:

I moved around a lot throughout my life and lived in a lot of different places. Each time, I had to learn the language, get used to local customs, and adapt to the education system (**broadly outlines experience, no specific example**). It was really challenging sometimes because I would accidentally offend people without meaning to and I struggled to make friends (**identifies challenge, but is focused on negative effects on self**). Eventually, I just got used to having to make these transitions all the time (**vague description of how challenge was overcome**), and now I'm very good at talking to people from different backgrounds because of my diverse experience (**identifies skill without future application**)

Strong response:

As a volunteer for Doctors Without Borders, I was sent to Cox's Bazar, Bangladesh with my team to provide medical care to the Rohingya refugees who have fled from Myanmar (**identifies specific experience**). Having to provide quality care to people from such a different and conservative cultural background was initially extremely challenging (**outlines the challenge**). One time, a young mother came into our tent with a high fever and conjunctivitis. We immediately suspected that it was the measles given that there was an outbreak at the camp, so I prepared her for a more thorough examination with the only physician on site at the time. However, upon realizing that he was a man, she refused to be examined. I then had to act quickly, convincing her to stay and wait while I got in touch with an off-duty female physician so that she could come in to examine and treat the young woman (**gives specific example**). During my two weeks there, I learned about and came to appreciate both the drastic and nuanced difference between our two cultures, and I developed ways to provide care to these patients while respecting their choices and cultural norms (**outlines how they proactively overcame the challenge**). I'm sure there will be many situations like this in my future career that will require me to set aside my own beliefs and habits in order to provide effective care to my patients and maximize treatment outcomes. This experience and others like it have prepared me to remain open-minded and adaptive to overcome the cultural barriers between me and my future patients (**clear future application**).

Discussion:

This is a personal type-question that asks candidates to identify a specific kind of challenge they had to overcome. As always for such a question, you must give a specific example that fits with what the question is asking, then discuss the ways in which you overcame that particular challenge, and what you learned. Many candidates will outline a general example, as you see in the *weak* response, without giving any details about a specific incidence where they were challenged. If you remain vague, it becomes extremely difficult to then describe how you overcame the barrier and connecting the process with skills or lessons you learned. In the *strong* answer, the candidate gives a tangible example of an interaction they had that illustrates the specific kind of barrier the question asks about. In doing so, they were able to expand on the exact way in which they dealt with that situation, before outlining what they learned and how the lesson is relevant for a medical professional.

16. Consider the following scenario: You are the only physician in the Emergency Department. You're about to get off your shift to pick up your 5-year-old son from daycare when several burn victims are rushed into your department in need of immediate attention. What would you do?

Weak response:

Since I'm the only physician in the department, it would be my responsibility to take care of my patients first, especially if they need immediate attention (**identifies one vulnerable party, but misses the other**). So, in this situation, I would treat the burn victims that came in (**presents one solution without gathering information about the situation**). I think it would be okay to delay picking my son up for a bit since the people at his daycare wouldn't just leave him there alone (**does not consider negative impact of actions on other parties involved**), but I would try to wrap up at the hospital as soon as possible so they're not waiting for too long.

Strong response:

As a physician of the Emergency Department, my primary concern is for the health of my patients, but as a father, I am also concerned and responsible for the wellbeing of my son (**clearly identifies dual role and both vulnerable parties**). In this situation, I would quickly assess whether the physician taking the next shift was already in the department and whether there were enough staff members on hand to take care of the burn victims and other patients needing immediate attention. I would also want to check to see if my spouse or another family member could pick my child up from daycare in my stead (**gathers information while acknowledging urgency of the situation**). If the next physician could readily take over and they do not need extra assistance with our patients, then I would entrust them with the care of these patients and go to pick up my child (**first if/then**). I would later call my department to make sure everything was okay (**continues to take responsibility for vulnerable party**). If the physician in the next shift had not yet arrived or my department was short-staffed, I would ask someone else in my family to pick my child up so that I could stay and help treat the patients (**second if/then**). If no one was available, I would at least inform the daycare of the situation and ask them to take care of my son for a while longer while I am delayed (**third if/then**). As soon as the situation eased up, I would make sure my patients are being properly taken care of and go to pick up my son to minimize the burden on the daycare staff. I would also offer to compensate them for their time (**acknowledging the impact on others**). Overall, my approach to this scenario would be to assess the situation and take action to ensure that my patients were receiving the treatment they needed and that my son was also being taken care of (**summary of approach**).

Discussion:

This is a scenario-type question that presents the candidate with a situation in which they simultaneously have two roles with differing priorities. The mistake made by the candidate who gives the *weak* response is that their answer is focused almost entirely on their responsibilities in one of these roles. They also failed to consider the impact of their choices and actions on others. Even though it is true that in this situation, the needs of the patients are greater, it is still important to take a balanced approach to any situation. The candidate who gives the *strong* answer is able to maintain this balance well by first identifying both of their roles and the differing pressing issues from each of those perspectives. They then work through the structure of the scenario (gathering information and hypothetical situations) while considering both sides. Ultimately this candidate presented a response that ensured the wellbeing of all vulnerable parties and even took into consideration the impact of their actions on parties that are indirectly involved.

17. Affirmative action policies have been enacted in colleges and universities to improve educational opportunities for minority groups. What are your thoughts on such policies?

Weak response:

There are probably a lot of reasons for universities to do this (**ineffective showing of awareness**). I think it's a great policy to have because I, myself, belong to a minority group, and there's been a long history of discrimination against my community (**takes an early stance without exploring PROs and CONs**). Policies like this give individuals like me a better chance at succeeding in academia and in future jobs as well (**cites personal gain**). If the policies had been enacted earlier, a lot of biases that exist in our society today probably wouldn't exist (**non-solution to the problem**).

Strong response:

From what I understand, affirmative action policies can come in different forms. For example, universities can reserve a certain number of spots of specific minority groups, or they can have lower acceptance thresholds for those groups. Either way, these types of policies are designed to benefit groups of individuals who have historically and systemically been discriminated against (**shows understanding of the policies and their purpose**). The policies give these groups more access to education, especially higher education, which also increases their chances of employment success. This then increases their visibility and representation in the work force, especially in privileged positions and professional roles, which encourages younger generations in their communities to break through barriers and achieve success (**PROs**). However, these types of policies have also been criticized for creating bias against majority groups. For example, several prominent universities have been sued for allegedly discriminating against Asian American applicants who are typically over-represented in student populations. Many of these students claim to have been denied entry into programs, despite having competitive applications, because spots are reserved for individuals from minority groups who may have slightly weaker profiles (**CONs**). While I agree that it is important to help minority groups overcome their barriers to education, I don't think they should do it in a way that introduces new biases into the candidate selection process (**takes a stance**). I think universities could instead offer these students access to preparatory resources such as academic tutoring or application preparation courses to help them become competitive candidates. During candidate selection, all applicants should be evaluated equally, regardless of their cultural or socioeconomic background (**outlines a modification**).

Discussion:

Quite obviously, this is a policy-type question. In order to deliver a strong response, you must first have a good understanding of the policies themselves. However, even two candidates who have the same level of understanding of a given policy can give responses that differ drastically in quality. In the *weak* answer, the candidate has a favorable viewing of the policy and therefore does not come off as judgmental. However, their response is overly biased to one side of the argument. Even worse, the reasons they cite in support of the policies in question are clearly driven by self-gain. In contrast, the *strong* answer presents a balanced approach. After demonstrating their awareness of the policies, the candidate gives a nuanced discussion of the pros and cons surrounding the policies and even cites a real example of when the policies became problematic. They then clearly stated their stance, after which they provided a solution that benefits both groups affected by the policies. Note that even though the policy structure does not call for you to state who the vulnerable parties are, your answer must still address them in the pros and cons and solutions you propose. Your considerations for policies should always be focused on those impacted by the policy beyond yourself.

18. Tell us about a dire situation you were in. How did you get out of it?

Weak response:

I have a severe peanut allergy, so I've always been cautious about what's in my food, but sometimes it's hard to control what others eat or carry around with them. Once, in third grade, a new transfer student brought a chocolate bar that contained traces of peanuts into our classroom. Immediately, the swelling started, and I felt my airway begin to close (**gives an example**). Luckily, my teacher was close by and helped me inject my EpiPen and called the ambulance (**describes how the problem was overcome**). She saved my life that day, and I'm really thankful for what she did (**shows appreciation, does not demonstrate lessons/skills learned or application**).

Strong response:

Last year, I went camping in Yosemite National Park with a few of my friends. On one of our hikes, we couldn't agree on which trail to follow, so we split up into two groups of two and took different paths. At the farthest end of our trail, my hiking partner took a wrong step and sprained his ankle, making him unable to manage the two-hour trek back to our camp site. As the trail was fairly remote, there were no other hikers, we had no cellphone reception, and it would be dangerous for us to be there past sun-down (**gives an example**). Thankfully, before we split up with our other friends, we had agreed on a rendezvous point and time. When we didn't show up, our other friends immediately contacted the park rangers and they were able to find us before anything worse happened (**describes how the problem was overcome**). This experience really taught me the importance of being prepared and making contingency plans in case things go wrong (**identifies what was learned**). It was a valuable lesson for me as an aspiring physician because doctors need to be able to foresee the many situations that can arise in their practice and mitigate undesirable outcomes (**clear application to medicine**).

Discussion:

This is another personal question that asks you to discuss a negative experience that you overcame. In the *weak* response, the candidate does articulate a clear example and how it was overcome. However, they selected an experience in which it is difficult to highlight any learning outcomes, let alone discuss how they might be applied. On the other hand, the candidate who delivers the *strong* response selects an experience where they could easily discuss an important lesson they learned that is relevant to the medical profession. They successfully outlined this in their answer.

19. Consider the following scenario: You are a lifeguard at your local beach. As you enter your shift, you notice that there are some empty beer bottles in the lifeguard hut where you're stationed. You check and find that they are still fresh, as if someone had just finished the contents. What would you do?

Weak response:

I know from personal experience as a lifeguard that when you're on the job, lives are at stake (**identifies a pressing issue**)! If I found empty beer bottles in the lifeguard hut, I would be very concerned that the previous lifeguard hard been drinking on the job and I would send an anonymous tip to the authorities right away (**makes assumptions and takes drastic actions without gathering information**). This is highly unprofessional behavior (**judgmental tone**), but more importantly, the safety and wellbeing of people who visit the beach should not be jeopardized under any circumstances.

Strong response:

As a lifeguard, my main concern is for the safety of the visitors to the beach, but I am equally concerned for the wellbeing of the previous lifeguard, my colleague (**identifies two vulnerable parties in the pressing issue**). Having discovered these beer bottles but not seen anyone drinking from them, I would not jump to conclusions since there is a lot of missing information (**remains non-judgmental**). I would thus, first want to contact the lifeguard on duty before me to ask them if they knew anything about the bottles and where they came from (**gathers information**). If I find out that my colleague confiscated the bottles from beachgoers violating open-container laws and disposed of the contents, then I would simply check with our supervisor to confirm that a report was filed regarding the incident. In this best-case scenario, my colleague was diligently fulfilling their duties and ensuring the safety of people at the beach (**first if/then, begins with best-case scenario**). If I discover that the beer belonged to the previous lifeguard and that they drank it on the job, then I would find an opportunity to discuss the matter with them privately (**second if/then, continues to gather information**). I would first ask them why they did this. If reveal to me that they were having personal issues, I would let them know that I was concerned for them and ask if there's anything I can do to help (**third if/then, showing empathy**). Regardless, I'd let them know in a non-judgmental way that consuming alcohol on the job compromises their ability to perform their job, in this case potentially putting lives at risk (**non-judgmental approach**). I would hope that this is a one-time lapse in judgment on their part, but if I find out that it's a recurring issue or that they do it again, I would have no choice but to report it to my supervisor to ensure that beachgoers are in good care (**fourth if/then**). Overall, in a scenario like this, I would first gather missing information without making any assumptions. If someone is at fault, I would first discuss the issue with them privately and offer my help if they need it, then report to higher authorities if it repeats or escalates (**summarizes approach**).

Discussion:

This is question that presents a situation with many unknown variables but is very suggestive of one particular hypothetical scenario. In order to successfully navigate this situation without coming across as judgmental, you must absolutely not make assumptions and jump to conclusions, as the candidate does in the *weak* response. Instead, use the scenario structure to guide you through, making sure to fill in the missing information gaps and entertain multiple scenarios, as the candidate does in the *strong* response. In doing so, you will be able to demonstrate your ability to consider a range of possibilities and respond appropriately to each.

20. What is one extracurricular activity you wish you had done as a child?

Weak response:

I did a lot as a child, so I probably wouldn't have had time to add anything else to my schedule (**avoids question**). I guess it would have been fun to learn a musical instrument (**identifies an activity**). A lot of my friends are musical, and growing up, they were always practicing, performing, or just jamming. Even though I enjoyed watching them play, I always felt a little bit excluded, so I think my time with them would have been more valuable if I knew an instrument myself and could participate (**cites self-serving reason, no discussion of a personality trait or skill, no application**).

Strong response:

As a child, my parents put me in a lot of extracurriculars such as drawing classes and piano, but I was never encouraged to participate in sports (**identifies activity**). While I enjoyed art and music, they were solitary activities that didn't give me many opportunities to engage with others. Therefore, I was very introverted until I was forced to come out of my shell in college (**identifies a problem**). Looking back, I think I would have benefited from participating in a team sport like soccer or basketball. Besides the obvious benefits this would have had for my fitness and physical health, it would have allowed me to exercise communication, collaboration, and even leadership skills early on (**describes how the activity would resolve the problem**). To make up for these lacking areas of mine, I made a huge effort at the beginning of college to join clubs that would allow me to socialize with my peers and work in a team setting. I even took up team rowing, which requires a great amount of coordination and communication with other rowers. Though I was sorely lacking in these skills before, I have worked hard to build them up in my adult life (**outlines what has been done to make up for what was lacking**). I know that physicians often work in teams and must communicate effectively with both colleagues and patients, and I am more ready than ever to take on this challenge (**application to medicine**).

Discussion:

This is a quirky question, but as with all other quirky questions, you need to treat it like a personal question. This means not only supplying the direct answer to the question, but also sharing a something about yourself with the interviewer that will help them assess the strength of your candidacy. This latter goal is not achieved in the *weak* response. The candidate identifies an activity but does not relate it to any personality trait, skill, or lesson they learned, thus missing the mark. In the *strong* response however, the candidate identifies a similar activity, but also a problem they had as a result of not engaging the activity. In this way, they were able to discuss what they have been doing since to overcome that problem, highlight important life lessons, and finally how these will be applied in their future profession. Remember, you must take every opportunity during the interview to show the interviewer that you are fit for a career in medicine; that includes quirky questions!

Now that you have had the time to try out these sample questions and read through our example responses and expert discussions, you should be getting comfortable with the strategies for each question type. In the next chapter, you will have further opportunities to practice what you know with 80 more questions. Before you begin, make sure you can identify the different question types and outline the correct approach to each. We will give you further instructions in the next chapter.

Happy practicing!

CHAPTER XIII

80 Practice Residency Interview Questions

N ow that you have familiarized yourself with the strategies for answering different types of questions and seen sample questions and expert responses, you can put your knowledge to the test!

This chapter provides 80 practice questions, including the three most frequently asked panel questions ("Tell us about yourself", "Why this specialty?", and "Why our program?"), as well as scenario, policy, personal, and quirky questions. Before you respond to a question, make sure you have identified the question type, then proceed using the appropriate structure. This will ensure that your answers are organized and comprehensive. If you need to review the question types and structures, please revisit *Chapter VII: Proven Strategies to Approach and Ace 6 Common Types of Residency Interview Questions*.

For the first few questions, write out an outline of your responses before practicing out loud. This will help you to be more confident with your use of the strategies. Later on, to make your practice more realistic, consider having a friend pose the questions to you as the interviewer. We also recommend that you begin recording your responses so that you can review them afterwards. This will enable you to track the length of your answers, your delivery, areas that need to be more concise, areas that need to be expanded or supplemented, red flags, and of course, your overall progress. To complete your practice, be sure to get objective, expert feedback either from a mature professional or by signing up for a BeMo preparation program. The expert will be able to point out areas in need of improvement that you missed and keep you on track as you work toward your goals.

A caveat: As you become familiar with the strategies and transitions, and get comfortable with certain personal examples, you may find that some of your answers begin to sound similar, or that you are using the same examples again and again. If this happens, it would be a good idea to take a step back and reflect on what other traits, interests, or experiences you could discuss to diversify your answers. Create a bank of these ideas that you can draw from with discretion and flexibility. Remember, it is very rare to encounter the *exact* same question twice. Therefore, it is normal and often necessary for the content of your answer to change as well. What should remain consistent each time is the structure, organization, and flow of your response, and the relevance of your points to the question.

Are you ready? Let's begin!

Interview Question 1

Tell me about yourself.

<u>What type of question is this?</u>

<u>What's the most pressing issue?</u>

<u>What is the best strategy?</u>

Interview Question 2

Why are you pursuing this specialty?

<u>What type of question is this?</u>

<u>What's the most pressing issue?</u>

<u>What is the best strategy?</u>

Interview Question 3

Why would you like to attend this program?

<u>What type of question is this?</u>

<u>What's the most pressing issue?</u>

<u>What is the best strategy?</u>

Interview Question 4

What is your approach to resolving conflicts?

<u>What type of question is this?</u>

<u>What's the most pressing issue?</u>

<u>What is the best strategy?</u>

Interview Question 5

What makes you angry?

What type of question is this?

What's the most pressing issue?

What is the best strategy?

Interview Question 6

Which organ in the body would you be and why?

What type of question is this?

What's the most pressing issue?

What is the best strategy?

Interview Question 7

If you had infinite time and money, what would you do?

<u>What type of question is this?</u>

<u>What's the most pressing issue?</u>

<u>What is the best strategy?</u>

Interview Question 8

Do you think vaccinations should be mandatory for children to attend public schools?

What type of question is this?

What's the most pressing issue?

What is the best strategy?

Interview Question 9

Name one challenge facing this specialty in the next 5 years and suggest a solution to this problem.

<u>What type of question is this?</u>

<u>What's the most pressing issue?</u>

<u>What is the best strategy?</u>

Interview Question 10

What is one thing you would improve about our program?

What type of question is this?

What's the most pressing issue?

What is the best strategy?

Interview Question 11

Tell me about a time you dealt with an uncooperative team member or colleague.

<u>What type of question is this?</u>

<u>What's the most pressing issue?</u>

<u>What is the best strategy?</u>

Interview Question 12

Consider the following scenario: You are a primary-care physician with a 75-year-old patient, Mr. Smith. You must tell Mr. Smith that due to his mobility and vision impairments, you are going to recommend to the provincial/state transportation authority that he can longer drive. How would you approach Mr. Smith? NOTE: You can also treat this as an acting station.

What type of question is this?

What theme(s) can you identify?

What's the most pressing issue?

What are the missing facts?

Who is directly and indirectly involved?

What are some hypothetical situations and solutions to each? Frame using the if/then structure.

Interview Question 13

What is your biggest limitation?

What type of question is this?

What's the most pressing issue?

What is the best strategy?

Interview Question 14

Do you think pass-fail or traditional numerical grades are best for assessing medical students?

<u>What type of question is this?</u>

<u>What's the most pressing issue?</u>

<u>What is the best strategy?</u>

Interview Question 15

Describe the image to the interviewer such that they can reproduce it without ever seeing the image.

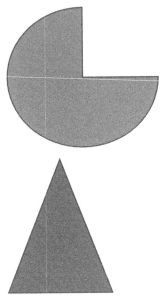

<u>What type of question is this?</u>

What's the most pressing issue?

What is the best strategy?

Interview Question 16

Reproduce the drawing below while answering the question "Why are you pursuing this specialty?" out loud.

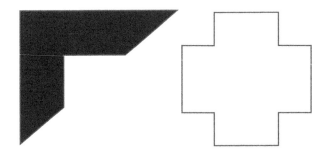

What type of question is this?

What's the most pressing issue?

What is the best strategy?

Interview Question 17

Consider the following scenario: You are a first-year resident. Your preceptor has been continually dismissive towards you, your colleagues, and even to patients. Today, while you were relaying a patient's history to him, he yelled at you for taking too long and called you an "idiot" in front of the entire team. How would you deal with this situation? NOTE: You can also treat this as an acting station.

What type of question is this?

What theme(s) can you identify?

What's the most pressing issue?

What are the missing facts?

Who is directly and indirectly involved?

What are some hypothetical situations and solutions to each? Frame using the if/then structure.

Interview Question 18

What was the most impactful experience you had during medical school? Please TYPE your answer in the next 4 minutes.

<u>What type of question is this?</u>

<u>What's the most pressing issue?</u>

<u>What is the best strategy?</u>

Interview Question 19

Some residency programs favor taking residents from certain geographical areas, such as rural ones, as they feel those residents are most likely to stay in the area after completing their training. What are your thoughts on these types of selection criteria?

What type of question is this?

What's the most pressing issue?

What is the best strategy?

Interview Question 20

Discuss a time when you had to master a new skill/technique quickly and teach it to someone else.

<u>What type of question is this?</u>

<u>What's the most pressing issue?</u>

<u>What is the best strategy?</u>

Interview Question 21

Teach me something in the next couple of minutes.

What type of question is this?

What's the most pressing issue?

What is the best strategy?

Interview Question 22

Which story would your friends tell us about you that would exemplify your personality?

What type of question is this?

What's the most pressing issue?

What is the best strategy?

Interview Question 23

Tell me about your research experiences.

<u>What type of question is this?</u>

<u>What's the most pressing issue?</u>

<u>What is the best strategy?</u>

Interview Question 24

Define empathy.

What type of question is this?

What's the most pressing issue?

What is the best strategy?

Interview Question 25

Consider the following scenario: You are a second-year resident. One day, a fellow resident, who you know well, tells you that she regularly posts images of patients on her social media pages. She posts these for what she claims are educational reasons and is aiming to build a following. What would you say to your colleague? NOTE: You can also treat this as an acting station.

What type of question is this?

What theme(s) can you identify?

What's the most pressing issue?

What are the missing facts?

Who is directly and indirectly involved?

What are some hypothetical situations and solutions to each? Frame using the if/then structure.

Interview Question 26

What is your greatest non-academic accomplishment?

What type of question is this?

What's the most pressing issue?

What is the best strategy?

Interview Question 27

Tell me about your time management skills.

What type of question is this?

What's the most pressing issue?

What is the best strategy?

Interview Question 28

Define patient-centered care.

What type of question is this?

What's the most pressing issue?

What is the best strategy?

Interview Question 29

What is your biggest failure?

What type of question is this?

What's the most pressing issue?

What is the best strategy?

Interview Question 30

Who is the most impactful mentor you have had? Please TYPE your answer in the next 4 minutes. NOTE: This can be used for a written station in MMI.

What type of question is this?

What's the most pressing issue?

What is the best strategy?

Interview Question 31

Although most physicians uphold high ethical standards, a small number slip up. One example is the potential abuse of the fee-for-service system used by most physicians to get compensated. Can you suggest one solution for this issue?

What type of question is this?

What's the most pressing issue?

What is the best strategy?

Interview Question 32

If you could have a conversation with any historical figure, who would it be? What would you discuss?

What type of question is this?

What's the most pressing issue?

What is the best strategy?

Interview Question 33

Describe the last medical journal article you read.

<u>What type of question is this?</u>

<u>What's the most pressing issue?</u>

<u>What is the best strategy?</u>

Interview Question 34

Tell me about a stressful experience and how you dealt with it.

What type of question is this?

What's the most pressing issue?

What is the best strategy?

Interview Question 35

What is something you are not looking forward to in practicing this specialty?

<u>What type of question is this?</u>

<u>What's the most pressing issue?</u>

<u>What is the best strategy?</u>

Interview Question 36

How would you approach a scenario where you are a senior resident and must break bad news to a patient concerning a terminal cancer diagnosis?

<u>What type of question is this?</u>

<u>What's the most pressing issue?</u>

<u>What is the best strategy?</u>

Interview Question 37

Consider the following scenario: A resident had some patient information, in the form of patient files and documents, in the trunk of his car. His car was parked in his parking garage but was broken into and the documents were stolen. What do you think should happen to the resident? Is he responsible for confidential documents getting taken?

What type of question is this?

What theme(s) can you identify?

What's the most pressing issue?

What are the missing facts?

Who is directly and indirectly involved?

What are some hypothetical situations and solutions to each? Frame using the if/then structure.

Interview Question 38

Discuss why leadership is important in a physician's career.

<u>What type of question is this?</u>

<u>What's the most pressing issue?</u>

<u>What is the best strategy?</u>

Interview Question 39

Tell me about a non-medical experience that taught you something important about being a physician.

What type of question is this?

What's the most pressing issue?

What is the best strategy?

Interview Question 40

Bed shortages and overburdened ERs are a part of modern medicine. Can you suggest two possible solutions to these problems?

What type of question is this?

What's the most pressing issue?

What is the best strategy?

Interview Question 41

When analyzing a complex problem, what steps do you take?

What type of question is this?

What's the most pressing issue?

What is the best strategy?

Interview Question 42

If you go unmatched, what will you do?

What type of question is this?

What's the most pressing issue?

What is the best strategy?

Interview Question 43

You are a student who borrows your friend's car and damages it on your way back from getting groceries. What would you say to your friend?

<u>What type of question is this?</u>

<u>What's the most pressing issue?</u>

<u>What is the best strategy?</u>

Interview Question 44

Which is more important, knowledge or information?

What type of question is this?

What's the most pressing issue?

What is the best strategy?

Interview Question 45

What is one healthcare issue you feel personally passionate about? Describe a program you would start to alleviate this issue.

What type of question is this?

What's the most pressing issue?

What is the best strategy?

Interview Question 46

Tell me about what you learned from a different specialty that is applicable to this one.

<u>What type of question is this?</u>

<u>What's the most pressing issue?</u>

<u>What is the best strategy?</u>

Interview Question 47

What strategies are you planning to use to combat the stresses of residency?

What type of question is this?

What's the most pressing issue?

What is the best strategy?

Interview Question 48

Which superpower would you choose to have?

What type of question is this?

What's the most pressing issue?

What is the best strategy?

Interview Question 49

Tell me about your experience using procedural skills. NOTE: Practice answering for common skills required in the specialty you are applying to.

<u>What type of question is this?</u>

<u>What's the most pressing issue?</u>

<u>What is the best strategy?</u>

Interview Question 50

What was your least favorite part of medical school?

What type of question is this?

What's the most pressing issue?

What is the best strategy?

Interview Question 51

Do you have ties to our geographical area? How do you plan on integrating to the community when you arrive?

What type of question is this?

What's the most pressing issue?

What is the best strategy?

Interview Question 52

What is your understanding of a multidisciplinary team?

<u>What type of question is this?</u>

<u>What's the most pressing issue?</u>

<u>What is the best strategy?</u>

Interview Question 53

What do you do to keep yourself busy?

What type of question is this?

What's the most pressing issue?

What is the best strategy?

Interview Question 54

Do you think patients have the right to question your practice?

<u>What type of question is this?</u>

<u>What's the most pressing issue?</u>

<u>What is the best strategy?</u>

Interview Question 55

What type of situation do you have the hardest time dealing with?

<u>What type of question is this?</u>

<u>What's the most pressing issue?</u>

<u>What is the best strategy?</u>

Interview Question 56

What are your plans for the next 5 to 10 years?

<u>What type of question is this?</u>

<u>What's the most pressing issue?</u>

<u>What is the best strategy?</u>

Interview Question 57

More than one in three low- and middle-income countries face both extremes of malnutrition, undernutrition and obesity. If you were a member of the World Health Organization overseeing this crisis, what steps would you take to help alleviate this issue and how would you prioritize these tasks?

What type of question is this?

What theme(s) can you identify?

What's the most pressing issue?

What are the missing facts?

Who is directly and indirectly involved?

What are some hypothetical situations and solutions to each? Frame using the if/then structure.

Interview Question 58

In what ways do you see yourself giving back to the community outside of your practice?

<u>What type of question is this?</u>

<u>What's the most pressing issue?</u>

<u>What is the best strategy?</u>

Interview Question 59

What are your thoughts on defensive medicine?

What type of question is this?

What's the most pressing issue?

What is the best strategy?

Interview Question 60

What would you change about the way candidates are selected for medical school and residency?

What type of question is this?

What's the most pressing issue?

What is the best strategy?

Interview Question 61

How do you manage simultaneous demands from work, family, and friends?

<u>What type of question is this?</u>

<u>What's the most pressing issue?</u>

<u>What is the best strategy?</u>

Interview Question 62

When do you feel most proud?

What type of question is this?

What's the most pressing issue?

What is the best strategy?

Interview Question 63

Teach me how to make your favorite dish.

What type of question is this?

What's the most pressing issue?

What is the best strategy?

Interview Question 64

What do you do when someone asks you for a favor you're unable to do?

What type of question is this?

What's the most pressing issue?

What is the best strategy?

Interview Question 65

Consider the following scenario: You are a resident in pediatric surgery. Once, you realize that you gave one of your patients a slightly higher dosage of post-surgery pain medication than what is recommended. You inform the surgeon you are working with right away, but they tell you that since it didn't have any negative impact on the patient's health, you don't need to report it or let the patient and their guardians know. How would you proceed?

What type of question is this?

What theme(s) can you identify?

What's the most pressing issue?

What are the missing facts?

Who is directly and indirectly involved?

What are some hypothetical situations and solutions to each? Frame using the if/then structure.

Interview Question 66

If you had the time and resources, what global health issue would you tackle?

<u>What type of question is this?</u>

<u>What's the most pressing issue?</u>

<u>What is the best strategy?</u>

Interview Question 67

What is your approach to mending a relationship?

What type of question is this?

What's the most pressing issue?

What is the best strategy?

Interview Question 68

What is the most promising new medical technology you've learned about recently?

What type of question is this?

What's the most pressing issue?

What is the best strategy?

Interview Question 69

A number of studies have reported that the majority of residents exceed their work-hour restrictions and/or that residents often underreport their hours. What are your thoughts on this?

What type of question is this?

What's the most pressing issue?

What is the best strategy?

Interview Question 70

What would you say are the pillars of professionalism for physicians?

What type of question is this?

What's the most pressing issue?

What is the best strategy?

Interview Question 71

What is another profession that you think would be worthwhile for you to pursue besides medicine?

What type of question is this?

What's the most pressing issue?

What is the best strategy?

Interview Question 72

When do you feel most vulnerable?

<u>What type of question is this?</u>

<u>What's the most pressing issue?</u>

<u>What is the best strategy?</u>

Interview Question 73

What would your friends say is your biggest change since starting medical school?

What type of question is this?

What's the most pressing issue?

What is the best strategy?

Interview Question 74

Consider the following scenario: You are a woman and the only physician on site in a remote area. An elderly gentleman comes into your clinic with what looks like serious injuries that need immediate attention, but he refuses to be treated by "a lady doctor". What would you do?

What type of question is this?

What theme(s) can you identify?

What's the most pressing issue?

What are the missing facts?

Who is directly and indirectly involved?

What are some hypothetical situations and solutions to each? Frame using the if/then structure.

Interview Question 75

Tell us about a situation where you were forced to do something you didn't want to do.

<u>What type of question is this?</u>

<u>What's the most pressing issue?</u>

<u>What is the best strategy?</u>

Interview Question 76

What are your thoughts on giving life-sustaining therapy when you judged that it was futile?

What type of question is this?

What's the most pressing issue?

What is the best strategy?

Interview Question 77

Describe a time when you advocated on someone else's behalf.

<u>What type of question is this?</u>

<u>What's the most pressing issue?</u>

<u>What is the best strategy?</u>

Interview Question 78

Do you think it's acceptable for physicians to prescribe a placebo to a patient if the patient insists on getting treatment?

What type of question is this?

What's the most pressing issue?

What is the best strategy?

Interview Question 79

What is a quirky skill you have?

<u>What type of question is this?</u>

<u>What's the most pressing issue?</u>

<u>What is the best strategy?</u>

Interview Question 80

What do you think will be your biggest contribution to the field of medicine?

What type of question is this?

What's the most pressing issue?

What is the best strategy?

Bonus Question

Do you have any questions for us? NOTE: This is a good place to make note of what you would like to ask the interviewers. Take this time to list the number of potential questions you could ask potential programs:

CHAPTER XIV

FREE Top Choice Match Challenge™

W e hope you enjoyed the book. We certainly have enjoyed teaching you what we know. As promised, we held nothing back and included everything we teach to our students in our interview prep programs found at BeMoResidencyInterview.com. We are confident that practicing with our strategies will take you a long way, but there is one missing piece of the puzzle we were not able to include in this book: expert feedback. In our experience, applicants improve the most when they take advantage of our realistic online mock interviews and get personal feedback from one of our experts. Of our successful students, 76% have participated in our interview preparation programs that provide this service.

Here is how our interview preparation programs work in 3 simple steps:

Step 1 - Top 5% experts: We pick the best experts for you. Our consultants work remotely, so we are not limited to a small talent pool in a narrow geographical location, and we can look for the best experts anywhere in the world. We screen dozens of M.D. and Ph.D. applicants every month. The multi-step application process is rigorous and involves a functional test, an online assessment, and an online panel interview with our senior team, including our CEO, Dr. Behrouz Moemeni. Only 5% of all applicants get hired, which means we are as selective with our candidates as many medical schools are with theirs. After new applicants are hired, they receive extensive training from our lead trainers, after which they continue to be monitored for 6 months before they become permanent members of our team. Our core team is thus composed of highly qualified, fully committed individuals who are there to support you through your residency application journey.

Step 2 - Expert private mentorship: Join us for a mock interview session and learn our proven strategies directly from one of our experts. Our experts will not only show you how to answer interview questions, make sound judgments, manage your stress, and communicate effectively, they will tailor the feedback to your unique needs by identifying your strengths and weaknesses. We are committed to teaching you skills that last a lifetime, not cheap tricks just to get around the interview.

Step 3 - Continuous rinse and repeat: Let us help you monitor your progress using a proprietary scoring system. We score students on multiple variables, including verbal communication, non-verbal communication, stress levels, ethical judgment, and so forth. This numeric scoring method gives us quantitative data so we can evaluate each student's performance objectively, rather than subjectively based on our fleeting impressions. You can continue to practice and receive feedback from our admissions experts until they are confident that you are 100% ready for your interview. Yes, that's right! Some of our programs include unlimited mock interviews with expert feedback!

BeMo's Bold Guarantees:

In case you're on the fence at all, we want to note that all our programs come with guarantees.

Go to BeMoResidencyInterview.com to learn more and enroll now or schedule a free strategy call to talk to one of our team members first.

Whether you decide to work with us or not, we hope this book helps you ace your interview, so you never have to go through this process again.

CHAPTER XV

Bonus Resources and Free Sample Residency Interview

Here are additional resources to help you prepare for your interviews.

Free online residency interview simulator via access to BeMo's revolutionary InterviewProf™ platform:

SampleResidencyInterview.com

Medical residency interview tips, strategies and sample residency interview questions

https://bemoacademicconsulting.com/blog/residency-interview-tips-strategies-sample-questions

The Ultimate Guide to CaRMS Interview Prep

https://bemoacademicconsulting.com/blog/carms-interview-prep

BeMo's sample MMI questions:
https://bemoacademicconsulting.com/blog/sample-mmi-practice-questions

BeMo's MMI prep blog:
https://bemoacademicconsulting.com/blog/category-multiple-mini-interview.html

How to Answer "Tell Me About Yourself" During Your Residency Interview:
https://bemoacademicconsulting.com/blog/tell-me-about-yourself-residency-interview

How to Create a Memorable Residency Letter of Intent
https://bemoacademicconsulting.com/blog/residency-letter-of-intent

Most Competitive & Least Competitive Residencies:
https://bemoacademicconsulting.com/blog/most-competitive-residencies

Navigating ERAS Application: The Definitive Guide
https://bemoacademicconsulting.com/blog/eras-application-the-definitive-guide

ERAS Timeline: The Absolute Best Timeline to Match to Your Dream Program:

https://bemoacademicconsulting.com/blog/eras-timeline

110 Best Residency Interview Questions to Know

https://bemoacademicconsulting.com/blog/the-five-residency-interview-questions-that-surprised-me

10 Common CaRMS Interview Questions and Answers

https://bemoacademicconsulting.com/blog/carms-interview-questions

Navigating CaRMS: The Definitive Guide to the Canadian Residency Matching Service

https://bemoacademicconsulting.com/blog/carms

ERAS Letter of Recommendation:

https://bemoacademicconsulting.com/blog/eras-letter-of-recommendation

International Medical Graduate: The Ultimate Guide

https://bemoacademicconsulting.com/blog/international-medical-graduate-residency

How to Write a Residency CV – The Definitive Guide

https://bemoacademicconsulting.com/blog/residency-cv

BeMo's private MMI test prep MasterMind Facebook Group:

https://www.facebook.com/groups/BeMo.MMIPrep.MasterMind/

Made in the USA
Las Vegas, NV
21 November 2023

81187590R00154